OUTSIDERS
A Journey to Belonging

DOREEN PADILLA

Barking Beagle
BOOKS

Outsiders : A Journey to Belonging
Published by Barking Beagle Books
Commerce City, Colorado

ISBN: 978-0-578-36294-6
BIOGRAPHY & AUTOBIOGRAPHY / Cultural, Ethnic & Regional / Hispanic & Latino

Cover and Interior design by Victoria Wolf, wolfdesignandmarketing.com. Copyright owned by Doreen Padilla.

DISCLAIMER: This book is the story of the author and to the best of her knowledge, the events shared are as they occurred. Many of the people in the book are named, with their agreement, and a few of the names have been changed to maintain privacy.

QUANTITY PURCHASES: Schools, companies, professional groups, clubs, and other organizations may qualify for special terms when ordering quantities of this title. For information, email barkingbeaglebooks@gmail.com.

Barking Beagle
BOOKS

This book is dedicated to my children.

May you pursue all your dreams with nothing holding you back.

Love, Mom

Just friends, right?

A NEW FRIEND

My freshman year of high school propelled me into culture shock. I was uprooted from the community I had known my entire life and dropped into unfamiliar surroundings that left me feeling isolated and invisible. Little did I know at the time that I would not only survive the experience, but it would shape my future in a way I could never have imagined.

I grew up in Commerce City, a suburb east of Denver. I was supposed to attend Adams City High School with all my friends I had gone to school with since kindergarten, but my parents had different plans for me and my brother, Dennis. My mother had grown up in Commerce City, and my father lived there as a child too. It had always been home for us. But my parents were vocal about their dreams of getting us out of there. That's how I found myself attending Arvada West High School, which is located just west of Denver, close to the foothills.

At that time, Commerce City did not have much to offer. It was small, the schools were some of the worst in the state, it was a highly industrial area, and it was home to many low-income households. Ever since I can remember, my parents took us to participate in sports or extracurricular activities in other cities because those activities were not available in Commerce City. So during my freshman year of high school, while we were still living in Commerce City, my parents drove my brother and me forty minutes each way to Arvada West High School every weekday morning.

Although Arvada was only a little more than fifteen miles away from Commerce City, I was shocked when I first walked into my freshman orientation. *Where did all these students come from?* I had never seen so many people packed into one gymnasium. We were all freshmen, and we filled the stands. As I looked around, it sunk in that I knew no one. Despite the roar of conversation around me, the world felt silent. I looked to my right, and there was a white girl around my age with blond locks and blue eyes. I looked to my left, and there was a white boy with brown hair and green eyes. I found myself lost in this sea of people, only to realize I did not look like anyone around me. I had dark brown hair and brown eyes, and my skin was tanner than usual because we were returning from summer break. My brownness stood out, and it was clear that I was not the only one who noticed. At that moment, I realized I was not in Commerce City anymore.

I scanned the crowd of kids and recognized that they were all dressed differently than me. What on earth was Abercrombie? It seemed all the beautiful girls sported that logo on their shirts, but I had never even heard of it. Where were all the Ralph Lauren and Tommy Hilfiger clothes? You know—the ones all the cool kids wore where I came from? I had lived my entire life less than an hour away, but this world could not have been more different from mine.

When I left orientation that day, I walked across the street to Walgreens. Although I had been to Arvada before, I did not understand where Arvada West High School was located or what was around it. When my mom dropped me off that morning, I remember scanning the neighborhood for something familiar. The only business I recognized was Walgreens. I caught myself daydreaming about how cool it was that I was in high school and I could leave the campus for lunch.

I walked around the perimeter of Walgreens, searching for a pay phone. When I found one, I called my mom at work to let her know I was done for the day. She answered the phone as her normal chipper self.

"Mom! They're all white!" I wailed.

"So?" she countered. "So are you!"

"But I don't look like them!"

Actually, my mom was white, and my dad was Hispanic. So my mom may have thought of me as white, but I did not look it. Commerce City had been primarily Latino, so in Commerce City, I looked like a white girl. Before coming to Arvada, I had never been considered a minority. I was in shock, trying to process what this meant for me now.

After the dust settled from orientation and the first few weeks of school, I started to settle in. I accepted that I was different. I did not look like everyone else, I did not dress like them, and I certainly had not grown up with the kind of money that most of the other students had. I had always attended Title I schools in which approximately 75 percent of students came from low-income families. The teachers often had pantries in their classrooms so students could take home snacks for the evening or weekends, and there was always support to help families navigate social programs such as food stamps and Section 8 housing. Going from a Title I school to a school in a mostly affluent neighborhood was not a scenario I had prepared myself for, but at age thirteen, I am not sure I could have prepared for that.

I was in Earth Science class when I met him. His name was Saul. Finally, someone who looked like me! When we started talking, I mentioned I had a birthday coming up. He curiously asked, "How old are you going to be?"

I was eager to answer. "Fourteen!" I exclaimed!

Saul looked at me with surprise. "Really?" he said. "I'm thirteen too!"

We were both young for our grade, and this fact felt familiar to me. Our birthdays were exactly three months apart, which would make it easy for me to remember his.

Like a magnet, I was attracted to him immediately—not in a romantic way but in the way someone seems familiar to you even without knowing them. He was quiet and bashful, and I was loud and ornery. Throughout that semester in Earth Science, I found myself wandering over to his table whenever I had free time. He would give me this little side smile while simultaneously showing annoyance with my pestering. I didn't let his annoyance faze me one bit. I loved his shy nature, and secretly, I could tell he liked my pestering. I cannot even begin to remember how many times our science teacher would yell, "Doreen! Get on task!" and I would quickly shuffle back to my seat. I would look over at him with my ornery smile, and he would just shake his head in disbelief and give me that cute side smile of his.

I soon realized we both had fifth period free. Unfortunately for him, he was stuck with me then, too, because neither of us had anywhere to go off campus during that time. Saul was not a big talker, but he was a good listener, and despite being annoyed by my persistence, he still hung out with me. We would walk the hallways during our free period when it was always so quiet in the school. Every now and then, we would run into his older brother, Dante. Dante also had fifth period free, but they never seemed to hang out during that time. Dante was a few years older than us. He was a junior, and to my surprise, he was even quieter than Saul. When we passed him in the halls during fifth period, Dante awkwardly acknowledged Saul, but he smiled at me. True to their quiet personalities, the two rarely said anything to each other.

After hanging out during fifth period and Earth Science for a while, Saul finally warmed up to me, and we would spend hours talking on AOL Instant Messenger and on the phone after school and on weekends. If he was on AOL Instant Messenger when I logged on, I was almost always the first to reach out.

"HIIIIIIIII!!!!!!!!!!" I would excitedly type, always over the top with as many exclamation points as I could fit on a line.

His response was always the same. "Hey!"

I took his single exclamation point as Saul's excitement to hear from me, too, even though it was much less enthusiastic than mine. In the early 2000s, chat rooms were becoming increasingly popular, and with them came the shorthand we see in texts and online now, such as WTF or ROTFLMAO. I could not stand it when people used acronyms or shorthand in their messages. Saul never used them, and it was an endearing quality.

Although cell phones were increasing in popularity, I did not have one. Saul did, which made talking on the phone that much easier. Once he had a cell phone, I never had butterflies-in-my-stomach anxiety about his family answering the home phone instead of him. So we spent hours on the phone together. He would ask how my day was, and I would always carry on about whatever drama was happening in my life at the time. That eventually led to us hanging out after school and on weekends too. One of our favorite things to do together was to go to the movies.

Saul had an older sister, Nina, who often drove us to the movies. Nina was the opposite of Saul and Dante. She was five years older than Saul, outgoing, beautiful, and certainly much more defiant than her brothers. She proudly drove a red Chevrolet Camaro, and you could see the tenacity in her eyes. I always offered to call Moviefone to see what was playing and check out the showtimes. I strategically told Saul about the romantic comedies first, knowing he would just go with whatever I wanted to see, despite his own preference for science fiction or action movies. That was just who he was—never one to make waves and always the type to just go with the flow.

The first time I went to Saul's house, I was taken aback by how quiet it was. He lived close to the school, in a bright orange house right off Sixty-Fourth Avenue, a busy street in Arvada. When I met his mother, Lizette, it was clear she did not speak English fluently. She was shy, like Saul and Dante. She was pleasant and warm but did not say much, only smiling and giving a small wave. Saul's home was so different from mine. You could hear a pin drop most of the time. His mom did not work outside the home, and her main role was to care for her children. Saul's father was always away at work.

Then there was Jorge, Saul's younger brother. Jorge was in middle school, so to Saul, he was just the younger, annoying brother. When he introduced me to Jorge, he simply said, "This is Jorge." Jorge gave me a slight nod but didn't speak and went right back to playing his video games. Saul whispered to me, "He's annoying. Just ignore him." Saul shared a bedroom with Jorge, who was even shyer than Saul and Dante, which was surprising to me. He wore glasses, liked to play video games, and never said much when I was around.

How could it be that their mother had three boys who were all so quiet and shy? It seemed like all the brothers were taught not to attract attention to themselves, and I wondered why. They could not be more different than my rowdy brother, Dennis, and Saul's relationship with his siblings was quite different from my relationship with my sibling. My brother and I were best friends and always together—so much so that Saul knew my brother pretty well too. I noticed that Saul was independent. He marched to the beat of his own drum, valued his friendships, and dedicated time to them. Instead of playing video games with his brothers, he spent his weekends and evenings with friends or playing soccer.

Saul's mom let us go into his room, just the two of us, with the door shut. We were only friends, but my parents would never have allowed that under any circumstances—just friends or not. I would sit on the bed and talk his ear off about God knows what was going on in my crazy teenager life, while he listened attentively. His nonverbal cues let me know he was listening. He had the darkest eyes I had ever seen; they were almost black. He looked into my eyes intently as I talked, never interrupting, rarely breaking eye contact. He was my favorite person to hang out with. My time with him always felt so easy.

FIFTEEN

Saul and I spent our freshman year getting to know each other. I spent many evenings and weekends on AOL Instant Messenger, typing away as I interacted with him. During the second semester, we did not have any classes together.

One evening, I messaged him enthusiastically with "I SAW YOU TODAY!!!" to which he calmly responded, "Okay, where?" Saul never replied with much excitement, but he always replied. Most of our conversations were casual, asking how each other's days were at school or what our plans were for the night or weekend. I vividly remember my mother yelling at me from across the house, "Are you still on the internet? It's time to get off! I need to make a phone call." This was back when you had to use the home phone line to use the internet. I always ignored her, pretending I didn't hear. She would wait a few minutes for me to follow through, but after it was clear I was ignoring her, she would come back to my room and look at the computer to see whose name was on my screen. Then she would tease me, saying I had a crush on Saul, and I would get defensive and yell, "No way!" She would shake her head and reiterate that I had been on the computer long enough.

I loved to hear the chime of AOL Instant Messenger, and Saul was consistently eager to talk to me there despite the insignificant nature of our conversations. AOL Instant Messenger was like the original social media. Saul always kept the same screen name—Saulinator, like *The Terminator*. I changed mine just about every other day. He always laughed at the new names, asking for the story behind them. One name seemed to particularly puzzle him. When I logged on as FrogInTheHotTub and sent my usual greeting, he replied, "Oh, it's you. What's with this new name?" I explained how that summer, I had gone on a trip with my father to Kansas, and when I was in the hot tub, my brother threw a frog on me. (Don't worry; the frog wasn't harmed.) Fourteen-year-old me thought it was funny and figured others would wonder about the meaning behind the name, so I kept it for a while. Our personalities could not be more different; he was always the calm to my madness.

We spent all summer together between our freshman and sophomore years. When I went to his house, we walked his cocker spaniels, Daisy and Donnie, to the lake a few blocks away. He eventually came to my house, too, and although my loud, crazy family could not be more different than his, he seemed comfortable there. Even after one full school year in Arvada, it still felt so foreign to me. I never quite felt like I could be myself at school, but Saul made me feel more at home whenever he was around. Not only did he have brown skin like me, but he was also kind and welcoming. In a school where I didn't fit in, he provided friendship and safety.

The fall of sophomore year put a halt to all the time we were spending together. Saul was a goalie on the soccer team, and I had been selected for the pom team that spring. I spent all summer at practice and camp, and during fall sports I had many activities to attend and less free time to spend with friends, including Saul. We both had frequent practices and games, but despite all the busyness of our extracurricular activities, we still found time to talk regularly on AOL Instant Messenger.

You could say I am nontraditional and a little forward because I took the initiative and asked Saul to be my date for homecoming that year. Over AOL Instant Messenger, I asked him, "Hey, if we don't end up having dates to homecoming this year, do you want to go together?" He paused before responding and finally replied, "Okay." Just like with all the times we went out to the movies together, he overcame his shy nature and reluctantly obliged.

Just before homecoming, I celebrated my fifteenth birthday and had all my closest friends over, including Saul. He wore a red polo shirt, and with his dark eyes, tan skin, and dark hair, he looked so cute. Saul could easily get lost in the crowd. He was never the loud or aggressive one, but I knew he was the loyal one. He was always there for me.

At my birthday party, I ended up hitting it off with one of my brother's friends, and we began dating. But, as planned, the weekend after my birthday, Saul and I went to homecoming together. I wore a beautiful red dress with a black rose-patterned overlay.

My cousin, Crystal, came over to help me get ready for the dance. She curled my hair and put it in an elegant updo on top of my head with a few loose ringlets falling below. I always had anxiety before events like this. Crystal and my mom unsuccessfully tried to calm me down as I panicked over not looking perfect enough.

When Saul arrived, I was feverishly searching through my messy closet for my purse. The rest of our party was already at my house when he arrived. My friends, Laura and Chelsie, and my cousin, Andre, were all there to take pictures together. They had already witnessed my anxiety and meltdown, so when Saul came walking up, they warned him that I was a mess. He came into my room, and it felt like all the fear and anxiety disappeared immediately. He gave me his cute side smile, and as always, it made me melt.

With his calm tone, he said, "Rough day?"

I giggled and said, "How did you know?" as I wiped underneath my puffy, red eyes.

"I had a hunch something was up," he said. "When I saw Laura and Andre outside, they suggested a couple of pickup lines I should use on you. But when I saw you, I figured it was best I don't use them. Wanna hear one anyways?"

I forced a tight smile. Saul knew better than to listen to my friends and my cousin, but I could tell it pained him to keep that line to himself. He just kept smirking.

"No, I don't want to hear it," I responded in a deadpan tone. He nodded his head in agreement and never repeated it within my earshot.

Saul wore a maroon button-up shirt that, like all the boys wore, was too baggy on him, with a white T-shirt underneath that was visible at the top of the shirt. He had longer hair, parted down the middle and slicked down on the sides. That was the style in the early 2000s, and to this day, his sister says he looked like a member of a boy band back then.

When I finally calmed down, we headed out to the front yard to take pictures. Although my cousin Andre went to a different school, he was my friend Laura's date, and he had met Saul at my birthday party the week before. They seemed to get along well; they were the only guys with the rest of us girls.

We all headed out to have dinner at a casual Mexican restaurant not far from the school. You would not expect to see a group of teenagers dressed in fancy clothes eating at this unassuming restaurant before homecoming. But Saul and I were not average teenagers from Arvada, and he embraced my willingness to be different.

When we arrived at the dance, the evening became awkward because my new boyfriend was looking on from afar, and I knew it. Saul was his typical happy self all night, dancing away with anyone who would dance with him. He knew my boyfriend was looking on, but he could not be bothered by it. Although this guy had been my boyfriend for only a week at that point, he was already demonstrating typical high school boyfriend behavior, full of jealousy and a desire to control. Saul would look at me, then track my eyes to see what I was looking at and see my boyfriend. Then he just shook his head at me in disappointment. Regardless, Saul had the cutest smile and truly danced like no one was watching, even though I knew they were. Every time he tried to get me to dance, I was too insecure and anxious to be present in the moment. It was so awkward to touch him, even for pictures. I think even the photographer could sense something was up, so instead of using the traditional pose where the couple is embracing, he had me sit in a chair with Saul standing behind me.

One thing was clear that night: our friendship had changed. My choice to date someone else left it more awkward and less easygoing. Saul and I stopped hanging out after that night. No more movies or visits to each other's houses. Eventually, our Instant Messenger chats ended, and we didn't talk on the phone. Once my best friend, he eventually became a stranger.

.

THE ART WALK

I struggled to fit in at Arvada West High School, regardless of how much time passed. I always felt like an outsider, like I was never one of them. I felt like my peers expected me to be perfect, and everyone there seemed disingenuous. I felt like my big, loud personality was too much for the people of Arvada. As a young woman, I was expected to be seen and not heard, to be polite and never make waves. Being a minority in a white school felt isolating.

When we took pictures for the pom team my sophomore year, no one wanted to sit by me in the team picture. One girl shouted, "Don't make me sit by her. I will look like a ghost!" Everyone laughed and engaged in the joke. They all said I was too dark and would make them look pale. As if I did not already know how different I was from them, it was a stark reminder that I was not the only one who noticed, and oddly enough, my dance coaches thought the dialogue was funny too.

Instead of hanging around for more humiliation, I ended up taking classes at the local community college during my last two years of high school instead of attending a traditional high school. I was still technically enrolled at Arvada West but did not go in person to the school unless I was forced to. This meant that I had not attended school with Saul since sophomore year. We reconnected at our senior prom two years later.

That boyfriend I had at homecoming two years before? Well, we happened to break up the night before my senior prom. We still agreed to go to prom together because we had already purchased the tickets and he had rented his tux. Looking back now, it almost seems like a story from one of the romantic comedies Saul and I watched together years before. Our senior prom was at Red Rocks Amphitheatre. It was underground and dark. I wore a beautiful magenta two-piece dress, but my eyes were swollen, and I could barely see because I had been crying for the past twenty-four hours.

I was feeling miserable when I heard a familiar voice say, "Doreen?" I looked back, and there was Saul. He was as handsome as ever. His slicked-back hair was even longer than before, and he was sharply dressed in a black tux. I was taken aback for a moment. Not only was I surprised that he would want to talk to me after our awkward experience at homecoming years before and our lack of relationship since, but I was equally surprised by the butterflies I felt in my stomach when I saw him.

Stop! I thought to myself. *It's Saul. You've always been just friends!* I quickly moved on to other thoughts. He had that same familiar gaze with that side smile. I was in a fog from my recent breakup, and everything felt surreal. I do not remember much from that night except for seeing Saul.

"Hi!" I finally responded.

"How have you been?" he asked. "I didn't know you still came to school here!"

I rolled my eyes a bit, not in a gesture of annoyance but more as an acknowledgment of the awkwardness of being at a high school prom for a high school where I was technically a student but did not attend.

"It's complicated," I responded. Saul just smiled at me. I said, "I have to go now," and we went our separate ways.

It had been so long since Saul and I were close friends that I no longer had his phone number, but this was in the days of Myspace. A week after prom, I searched for Saul on Myspace and sent him a friend request. I could not have been happier when he accepted my request. He will tell you how surprised he was to see it too.

We picked up right where we left off. Instead of talking for hours on end on AOL Instant Messenger, we now had cell phones, and texting was becoming popular. Everything felt so comfortable and familiar again. I asked Saul if he wanted to go to the movies and see *The Break-Up*. He said sure, but he would need a ride.

When I picked him up, I asked, "Does one of your brothers have your car?" After a small period of silence, he responded.

"I don't have a car. I don't drive," he said.

I was perplexed. I had friends who shared cars with their siblings or their parents, but they all, at a minimum, had their driver's licenses. Despite my curiosity, I did not inquire any further. I figured if there were more to it, he would let me know.

Saul was planning to go to Regis University in the fall, and I was going to Red Rocks Community College while working as a hairstylist. When Saul went off to school, we once again disconnected. There was no reason for the distance between us this time—no big fight or disagreement over a new boyfriend—and we would reconnect here and there over the years to check in and see how each other was doing. I got married, had a baby, and was divorced, all by the time he was done with his bachelor's degree in biochemistry. I guess you could say I was busy.

One of the times we reconnected was on his twenty-first birthday. His birthday was exactly three months after mine, and we were both ending relationships and in the beginning phases of dating new people. It was a Thursday evening, which meant it was Thirsty Thursday at the Sports Column bar in the LoDo neighborhood of downtown Denver. I was not one to go out much, despite only recently turning twenty-one, so I was excited to dress up and go out. I wore one of my favorite dresses, an ombre-style, color-block dress in black, charcoal, and silver. My hair was styled in a short, brown A-line.

I arrived and saw that Saul was dressed in a blue checkered button-up shirt, and his hair was much shorter than it was the last time I saw him. He was already three sheets to the wind by the time I showed up. Instead of his usual shy side smile, he was much less reserved. He gave me the biggest hug he had ever given me, and he had the biggest smile on his face. I quickly joined him, downing shot after shot. Then we found ourselves on the dance floor. Saul was still willing to dance, just like at homecoming so many years before. The difference this time was that I was willing to dance too. Sports Column was somewhat of a dive bar, but it had a dance floor, nonetheless. A few people were on the dance floor with us, but we were in our own world, just the two of us. Despite my level of intoxication, I remember that evening like it was yesterday. Saul and I were bumping and grinding, something we had never done before. If any previous level of attraction existed, it had been kept subdued. As we were dancing, I remember Saul put his hand on my hip, and it was in all his drunken glory that he yelled into my ear, "Why do you have to have a baby?"

Why do you have to have a baby? It was like the bar went completely silent and time stood still when he asked me that question. I couldn't believe Saul said that. He had never said anything like that to me before and, well, I couldn't blame him. The mutual attraction that evening was clear, but Saul and I were in totally different places in our lives. We were twenty-one years old, and I was recently separated from my husband with a one-year-old baby girl. Saul was in college with little responsibility. He did not work and had to focus only on his studies. We had one last shot of gin with his friends, and we both headed our separate ways.

Following his birthday, I called him every few months or so to check in. He never called me first. My first question was always, "How's the love life?"

He often responded that it was nonexistent or had just ended. He says my timing was always impeccable; I always called him just as a relationship was ending. My opinion is that he never kept his girlfriends long enough for me to meet them. Over the years, I never forgot his birthday, and if you ask him, he will tell you I was always the first to wish him a happy birthday every year.

Saul graduated from college summa cum laude, winning the American Institute of Chemist Award at Regis University at the age of twenty-one. He majored in biochemistry with a minor in French and biology. This was in 2010, shortly after the economic recession that hit the United States hard in 2008.

After graduation, Saul seemed to struggle to find his way. Every time I asked about his job status, he said he was working odd jobs here and there, "promos," as he called them. He worked events like the National Western Stock Show or Taste of Colorado for various vendors. I remember wondering why he was struggling so much to find work, considering he had a degree. I never asked him why he was working these odd jobs. I did not want to offend him if that was what he really wanted to do after college. It was odd to me that he was not working full time, nor was he using his degree. I often paused to wonder what was going on with him professionally, but I always quickly moved on, assuming it was just a result of the poor economy from the recession and his lack of professional work experience.

Saul and I finally reconnected in person when we were twenty-five. Tired of the phone calls, I suggested we meet for dinner. I was no longer dating anyone, and neither was he.

In my early twenties, I developed a love for fitness. About any day of the week, you could find me working out at the gym, which was just up the street from Saul's house, so it was convenient to find a time and place to get together. We agreed to meet at Chipotle before my group exercise class one Wednesday evening. This would be the first time I saw him in four years.

Saul was not on social media whatsoever anymore, so I had not even seen how he had changed over the years. He had just gotten off work, so he was dressed professionally. Seeing him for the first time in so long felt different. His hair was parted down the side with a fresh fade and styled perfectly. His style was more put together than I had ever seen before, from his choice of a button-up shirt to his matching belt and dress shoes. I am not exaggerating when I say I was speechless. Saul and I had one moment on his twenty-first birthday years before when the attraction between the two of us was undeniable, but I chalked that up to the alcohol and told myself he was my friend. This time, things felt different. He even looked at me in a new way. His side smile was familiar, but it was warmer and bigger. Since I was also coming from work, Saul saw a different side of me too. I was wearing heels and a white dress accented with black flowers.

Saul smiled big and said, "You look really nice!"

I can remember that comment kicking up butterflies in my stomach. I thought to myself, *What's with these butterflies again?* As we visited over dinner, I asked him what he had been up to.

"I'm interpreting in the medical field now," he excitedly explained.

I could see a twinkle in his eye like I had never seen before. I asked, "What does that consist of?"

"I go to medical appointments with patients who have workers' compensation claims and help them navigate their appointments, since many are not fluent in English," he explained. The way he lit up when he described helping others navigate the health care system was charming. He had always been patient, kind, and smart, so I should not have been surprised that he would want to help people for a living and would be good at it, but it was intriguing to me. I explained that my mom worked with workers' compensation claims, too, but from the human resources perspective. It was endearing to hear him talk about the work from his perspective.

The conversation shifted gears a bit. "Thank you for meeting me here! I work out at the gym right there," I said as I pointed to the building right behind Chipotle.

He looked it over and said, "Oh really? How is it?"

"It's great," I replied. "I do kickboxing and high-intensity interval workouts, which are called HIIT. In fact, after this, I am going to do a HIIT workout!"

His eyes widened, and the expression on his face changed. "You're going to work out after this?" He seemed surprised.

Although I never ate a big meal before working out, I wanted to see him but also did not want to miss a workout. "I have to!" I exclaimed and winked at him. I never missed a workout for a guy. It was a rule I set for myself, but I also never decided to eat before a workout either. Saul was special enough to me that I would find a way to make both work.

The tone of our conversation that day was certainly friendlier than our recent phone conversations. He was more outgoing than when we were younger, and I was more forward too.

Saul and I didn't wait as long to see each other the next time. Instead of years between in-person visits, it became only a month or two. We had a few dinners together, and each time I felt butterflies. I could no longer chalk up the attraction to a fleeting thought. It was clear I had feelings for him. Even my colleagues knew I had a crush on the man who was once my best friend. My friend Jose told me I should tell Saul about my feelings for him. "After all, you only live once!" he declared. Jose was a hopeless romantic. In contrast, I also told my friend Paul, who told me to take that secret with me to the grave because "Sometimes friends are meant to be only friends." For the time being, I kept my feelings to myself.

The following spring, I had a job offer in Baltimore. Saul was also on a new journey; he had been accepted into the Teach for America program. He was heading to Tulsa, Oklahoma, that summer to train to be a teacher and did not know where he would land after that. I was apprehensive about going to Baltimore, and I asked Saul what he would do if he were me. He said, "Well, I am taking a big risk this summer. I think you should too." He gave an honest answer, and I felt a little crushed by his honesty. If he cared about me, too, he would in no way tell me to move all the way to the other side of the country.

Summer came, and I bailed on the job opportunity in Baltimore. There were just too many variables I could not commit to. Saul still went to Tulsa, and we checked in a few times while he was there. He was enjoying himself, but he was busy too. Every time my phone rang and I saw his name, I felt butterflies. I remember thinking to myself, *What in the world is going on with these butterflies?* I had dated plenty—probably too much—but I could always drop those guys pretty easily and never had feelings like these. I took note of the butterflies but quickly dismissed them, knowing he probably did not feel the same way. One evening, he called me, excited to share the news that he was being placed in Denver to teach in the fall. I was so excited to know he would be back. We made plans to hang out on August 1.

When August 1 came around, Saul was living in the Baker neighborhood in downtown Denver. In all the years I had known him, he was either living at his parents' house or in a dorm. I was excited for him. He was living with two roommates he met through Teach for America. Our plan for the evening was to meet at his house so I could see the new place. Then we would walk to dinner at Spicy Basil and go across the street to an independent theater to see the film *Boyhood*.

In all the recent times Saul and I got together, I was just leaving work and was dressed in heels and a dress. This time, I thought I would dress more casually but "cute casual." I wore jeans with a fitted tank top underneath a loose-fitting white tank. I wore gladiator-style flat sandals. My skin was bronze, just like it had been in the summers during high school, but I had recently colored my hair a bright red. I remember thinking, *I wonder what he will think, seeing me like this?*

When I arrived at his home, I immediately took note of how unique it was. It was an old brick bungalow that had been remodeled. Parking was scarce on the street, and the sidewalks were ridden with cracks and weeds growing through. Inside, his bedroom was the largest and at the back of the house. Some of the walls featured exposed brick, and the kitchen had been remodeled to be open and spacious. It was a stylish home with lots of character.

Next, we walked to Spicy Basil. I was not a fan of that type of food, but I could never tell Saul that because he chose the restaurant. So I found something on the menu I could try. Throughout dinner, I remember looking into his dark eyes. They were the familiar eyes I had known for so many years. I could look into them forever, but of course, I didn't want to make things weird.

We had a lot to catch up on that evening. The last time we saw each other, I had been considering moving to Baltimore and he was going to Tulsa for Teach for America.

"So, why did you decide to stay here after all?" he asked.

I smiled, not entirely confident that I even knew the answer to that question. "It seemed far too complicated for me to leave at the time, especially to go that far away from home," I explained. "So, how was Tulsa?"

Saul nodded and smiled. He quickly caught on that I was not interested in talking about Baltimore anymore. "Tulsa was a whirlwind!" he said. "I have never been that busy in my entire life."

We went on to talk about the various experiences we had over the summer and the hopes we had for the future. The conversation flowed so naturally that we missed our planned movie time. Since we missed the movie, we decided to head over to the Santa Fe Art District for the Art Walk. It was the first Friday of the month, so Santa Fe Drive was lined with open art galleries, exhibitors, food trucks, and people.

As Saul and I walked through the art exhibits, we continued our conversation. After walking out of the first exhibit, Saul looked at me with his cute side smile and said, "I never realized how short you are."

I giggled and said, "You didn't? After all those years hanging out together?"

"You were always in heels, and this is the first time since high school that I've seen you in flats." Our hands kept grazing as we walked closely together, and I kept awkwardly apologizing.

We talked about our summers, our lives, and our hopes for the future. I told Saul about a book I had read that summer called *Just Like Us: The True Story of Four Mexican Girls Coming of Age in America*. It was about four young girls from Denver who were all undocumented and going through high school, trying to find their way and figure out how they would one day go to college.

"This book was life-changing for me. You have to read it!" I told him enthusiastically. "I always thought I understood immigration, but I realized I know very little. I can't believe all that these young women had to face at such a young age. It made me see immigration very differently."

Saul listened attentively and nodded gently but did not offer much response.

I went on, "This one girl was not even sure if she would be able to go to college, so she almost gave up on her studies in high school. I can't imagine. I probably would have given up if I were them."

Saul again nodded in agreement and said, "Those are good stories to read. I wish more people knew about stuff like this."

That evening, we walked back to his house, where my car was parked. We did not go inside. Instead, we hugged, and I went on my way.

On my drive home that evening, I knew something was different this time. Saul and I always had a unique connection. Over the years, I had many friends, both male and female, but with Saul, things were always so easy. Not only did we not have conflicts, but he also had a way about him that made me feel safe and calm. We had an obvious attraction, like a gravitational pull to each other, but I always felt scared of losing what I had with him. So I continuously reminded myself that he was just my friend and there were no romantic feelings. Despite feeling that our relationship was more, I was too scared to mess it up and never wanted to take a chance.

Saul may not have romantic feelings toward me, but he keeps coming back for a reason, I thought. My mind raced with thoughts of our conversations that night and just how much chemistry I felt with him. Although we always connected in ways I did not connect with others, this time, it felt like we connected on a deeper level than before. I knew it was time to be more forward, and if he wasn't interested in me romantically … well, at least I would know I had tried. If I were the one reading the room wrong that evening, I would soon know and could find a way to move forward as friends like we had always been in the past.

FIRST KISS

fter the Art Walk, I could not ignore my feelings for Saul anymore. The butterflies intensified every time I saw my phone light up with a text notification from him. The conversations had changed by this point, and the texts had a flirtier tone to them now. I vividly remember one text exchange. I had bought a dress for my brother's upcoming wedding. The dress was a beautiful, floor-length lace gown with an open back. I felt confident in the dress, and I decided to send Saul a picture of me in it. Saul and I had never had a history of sending photos to each other, and I can remember staring at the text for a solid five minutes before finally finding the courage to tap the send button. I wanted to see how he would respond—to see if there was any ounce of flirtation or attraction there. The butterflies intensified when he responded with, "You look beautiful." Oh. My. God. I took note that he did not say the dress was beautiful; he said I was beautiful. I was a bundle of nerves back then, anxiously waiting for the next phone call, text, or visit.

Saul had a few weeks of summer left before he would begin his first teaching job in September. I was in between jobs, with my new job starting on September 2, so we both had a lot of free time. He invited me to the Denver Zoo for an exclusive show just for teachers. I was too into him to admit that I absolutely hated the zoo—something about the smells and caged animals never sat well with me. We planned to meet at the zoo on a Saturday afternoon.

I have always tended to overbook myself, and this day was no different. That morning, I was running a half-marathon from Georgetown to Idaho Springs, about an hour west of Denver in the mountains. I left myself with little time to get ready before I met Saul. I finished the half-marathon a sweaty mess and raced back home to shower and head to the zoo. Every time I saw Saul, I meticulously thought out my entire look. From my outfit and accessories to my makeup and hair, I always wanted to be perfect when I saw him. This time, because I overbooked myself, as I'm known to do, I had no time to truly get ready. I did not tell Saul that I was busy that morning. I threw my hair into a side braid, put on a dress and minimal makeup, and rushed to get there on time.

I wore a fitted, coral-colored maxi dress that always generated compliments. It flattered my figure but also looked great against my tan skin from the morning run. I was not feeling confident that day because I did not have the time to look perfect, but I will never forget the look on Saul's face when he saw me. That familiar side smile was replaced by the biggest smile the moment he saw me.

As we walked around the zoo, Saul casually asked, "How was your morning?"

"I ran the Georgetown-to-Idaho Springs half-marathon this morning," I said. "How was yours?" I didn't think much of that achievement, but his response made me proud.

He looked at me and said, "Really? I don't know how you did all of that this morning, and you are not in bed right now!"

I laughed flirtatiously and said, "I wouldn't miss an opportunity to hang out with you."

As we continued to walk through the zoo and talk about how our week went and our plans for the upcoming week, he randomly paused and smiled at me.

He said, "I still cannot believe you are here right now. I am so impressed by you."

Saul was no longer that shy guy I once knew. Not only did he seem much more confident now, but he was also much warmer and more complimentary of me.

That afternoon at the zoo, we attended the exclusive show for teachers and their families. Saul said he was not sure what the show would consist of but that teachers were highly encouraged to come and learn about the animals. I was shocked to find out it was a bird show. Saul never knew this about me, but I am terrified of birds. How on earth could I tell him that now? I was feeling indescribably vulnerable at that moment. I am petrified of birds, let alone birds flying above my head and from all sides. So I never told him. I sat there with him, my heart racing from the birds flying everywhere and also from the butterflies flying around in my stomach, reacting to another date with Saul. *Wait, was this a date?* It felt like it.

I somehow survived the bird show without Saul ever knowing how scared I was. On our walk back toward the car, it started to pour down rain. We ran into the closest bathrooms on the zoo grounds, him in the men's and me in the women's. My heart was pounding from running. I sat down on a bench in the bathroom and took a deep breath. I thought of Saul, sitting right next door, drenched from the rain too. Our conversations over the past few weeks felt different. I had finally stopped trying to convince myself that he was just my friend and that my feelings for him were platonic. I was romantically attracted to Saul. I thought he was handsome, smart, and charming, and there was no denying it. So the only question now was how he felt about me. It seemed as though the rain lasted forever, and I wanted nothing more than to be with him again. We waited out the rain that probably lasted only ten minutes or so and then met outside and finished walking to the car.

I am probably the most awkward person ever to hug. My friends have even described me as a cactus. I never know if it's supposed to be a full-frontal hug or a side hug, and I overthink it. I awkwardly hugged Saul when we arrived at my car and quickly got into the driver's side. To avoid making things awkward, I made them even more awkward with my quick hug-and-run. This was common for me. I did it every single time with Saul.

To my surprise, Saul invited me over for dinner the following week. He did not want to go out but instead wanted to cook for me. I went to his house, and he had a spaghetti dinner already prepared. He also invited one of his roommates, Paul. We all sat down at the dinner table to eat and enjoyed a good conversation. Then Paul left us alone, and we continued to talk.

At the end of dinner, I attempted my quick hug-and-run like I had always done in the past, but this time, Saul changed the narrative. He asked me to stay and watch a movie with him. I was excited to spend more time with him, and somehow a movie with Saul felt all too familiar. We sat down on the couch to watch the movie. I cannot even remember what movie it was because my thoughts were constantly racing that night. *Am I sitting too stiff? Am I sitting too close? Should I move closer?* I could not, for the life of me, relax and just be in the moment. About twenty minutes into the movie, Saul put his arm around me and pulled me in closer. This intensified the thoughts and butterflies. I was so perplexed. *What did any of this mean?* Despite all my feelings for him, I was never sure of his feelings for me.

About ten minutes later, he finally leaned in and kissed me. *Holy shit! What was that?* Not an ounce of awkwardness in the kiss. Suddenly, I was no longer confused about Saul's feelings for me. He kissed me! Something I had daydreamed about and hoped for, for so long. When I prepared to leave that evening, Saul kissed me goodbye. It was late, and it was dark. I had about a thirty-minute drive home from his house, and my mind was racing the entire time.

DATING

After our first kiss, Saul and I began spending more time together. He was the most romantic and thoughtful person I had ever dated. We explored Denver in ways neither of us had ever done before. We attended Taste of Colorado, went ice skating, and visited vintage ice cream shops all around the city. After a few weeks, we reflected on how nice it was to explore together instead of alone.

We visited a Mexican restaurant in his neighborhood that looked to have a romantic vibe to it. We had both noticed it the evening of the Art Walk and thought it looked intriguing. At the center of the outdoor seating was a gorgeous water fountain with colorful tiles. It was clear this was the focal point of the entire restaurant. One gorgeous late summer evening in Denver, we decided to go. The air had a slight chill to it as the sun went down, and Saul and I sat on the patio, listening to the sounds of the water flowing through the fountain. I could not help but look into his dark eyes and think, *How did I get so lucky, and why the hell did it take so long?*

As the evening wore on, a mariachi singer began to serenade all the guests, accompanied by beautiful music from his guitar. He made his way to our table and asked what song we would like. Saul and I looked at each other, and I just smiled. I had no idea what song to choose. Saul smiled back at me, looked at the man, and said something in Spanish I did not understand. The man smiled and began singing. Even without knowing Spanish, it was clear the song was romantic. The one word I did understand was "luna." Luna is moon in Spanish. The ambience quickly became even more romantic as Saul placed his hand on my leg and gave me that sweet side smile so familiar to me.

I was a little surprised by Saul when he chose the song. He was confident and quick to respond to the musician's question. I knew Saul was fluent in Spanish. After all, when I visited his parents' house, he would often speak Spanish with his mother. But in this moment, I was a bit taken aback. He knew exactly what song to request; it seemed perfect for the occasion. Saul was not from the United States—he was born in Mexico—but he never really talked about Mexico or his culture. I knew he was from Mexico only from what I saw on MySpace when we were younger. There was a space for entering your hometown, and Saul had entered Durango, Mexico. Except for past visits to his childhood home, this was the first time I had witnessed Saul surrounded by his culture. There was Mexican food, Mexican décor, Latin ballads, and couples dancing to the music all around us. Saul seemed at home and comfortable. When I was speechless with the musician, Saul knew exactly what to say.

Unfortunately, we didn't enjoy the food at this restaurant as much as we did the ambience. When we were preparing to leave that evening, I asked Saul what he thought of his meal. He hesitated, made an awkward face, and said, "I was not a big fan. What did you think?" I could tell he was being polite because he was not sure what I thought of mine. For him to say he was not a fan seemed out of the ordinary for him, so he must have thought it was pretty bad.

I giggled because I was not impressed by the food either. "Yeah, I think we have many better options around Denver that we can choose if we want Mexican food."

Saul laughed too. "I'm glad we are in agreement. Let's not go there again."

So even though it provided the setting for a romantic evening, this restaurant did not become one of our favorites.

Saul and I jumped into dating quickly, from seeing each other once every few months to often going on dates and doing new things together. We talked every day, and at first, we were just enjoying each other's company. But on my birthday in mid-September, we finally agreed to be in a committed relationship. It was crazy to think about. Saul and I met when we were thirteen years old. Now it was twelve years later, and here we were, more compatible than I could have ever imagined, and the physical attraction was undeniable too. We kept our relationship to ourselves at first, just the two of us.

While we were dating, I learned a lot about Saul. I learned that he spent some of his childhood in California but that he was indeed originally from Mexico. He always seemed to move on quickly from the conversation when we discussed Mexico, and I always wondered why. So one day, I asked him, "So, when did you move to the United States?"

His response was short. "Right before my second birthday." He was to the point, he answered the question, but he added no more details.

I inquired further. "How often do you go back?"

He said, "I never have." His responses almost sounded cold for Saul. He was always a little more on the introverted or shy side, but he seemed to be even more so when this topic came up.

So I pressed further. "Even with your grandparents getting older?"

At this point, it was clear I had asked a dumb question, but he respectfully responded with, "They used to come visit here more often, but as they got older, they stopped."

I could read his body language. He was not interested in discussing that time of his life in detail with me. I was baffled by it, but I figured he would share more when he was ready.

We talked about his experience attending Regis University to study biochemistry and what it was like to have that true college experience. I could not relate to the college scene. I had continued on at the community college where I took classes in high school, but I dropped out after the first year. I had recently gone back to school a few months before we started dating, attending Colorado State University online full time while also working full time.

These commitments worked out okay for us because we would spend many Sundays in the study rooms at Regis, me studying and writing papers while he planned for his classes the upcoming week and graded his students' work. We took breaks every now and then and walked around the campus. I got to know a different side of Saul on these walks. He was so open with me and willing to share his experiences and thoughts. He showed me where his dorm was, where his classrooms were, and my absolute favorite—the St. John Francis Regis Chapel. The chapel is indescribable and breathtaking. When you walk in, natural light shines through the wall of windows ahead. You can see the foothills west of Denver through the windows, and the natural wood accents add to the clean feel of the sanctuary. The first time Saul showed me the chapel, I thought to myself, *I hope I marry you here one day.* It was far too soon to share that with him, but everything felt so natural and easy that I was hopeful he would one day want to marry me.

In October, he took me to a barbecue to meet his friends from college. His friends Brittany and Alex were going to medical school in Denver and were hosting the get-together at their home. Another friend, Gabe, attended too. He was also going to medical school in Omaha, Nebraska. Their friends Vinnie and Sean were not able to make it there. One of them was going to dental school and the other to medical school. I remember feeling so insecure as I met all his friends—all pursuing advanced degrees in medical or dental school—and here I was just working on my bachelor's degree. My saving grace was that I was working at a hospital at the time, so I could fake my way through the conversations, hoping they would not ask where I went to school or what exactly I did at the hospital.

Brittany was warm and friendly, with a calm demeanor like Saul's. She made me feel comfortable despite my insecurities. Although internally, I was terrified of what they would think of me—a young single mom just now going back to school—she made me feel welcome and included.

As the night progressed and the friends reminisced about the great times they had together in college, they all agreed that Saul was the smartest of them all. They seemed surprised that Saul did not continue on to medicine as they had. They were not judgmental in any way but genuinely perplexed by the path he chose to take.

Later that evening, I reflected on previous conversations with Saul. I remembered him talking about going to pharmacy school after he graduated from Regis, but he never followed through with that. I didn't think much about it at the time. I had not even finished my bachelor's degree, so who was I to question someone for not continuing their education? But after meeting his friends and hearing about their experiences with Saul in college, I began to wonder why he didn't pursue an advanced degree. He was obviously smart enough. I, too, found myself perplexed by Saul's decisions. While his friends were talking about their college experiences and preparing for medical school, and while they mentioned the fact he did not continue his education, he remained present in the conversations—never defensive or excited—but with limited participation. He would just smile and humbly disagree when they said he was the smartest of them all.

That November brought a big ballot initiative related to public schools. The initiative would provide salary increases to staff and more resources for teachers in the classroom. I had never voted; I was not even registered to vote. I thought voting was a waste of time and a pain to do. I thought, *What does my one vote do?* Saul had a way of challenging my stubbornness, sometimes causing me to roll my eyes at him, but regardless, I always heard him. That November, he encouraged me to vote and was persistent in why it was important to do so regardless of my complaints about the inconvenience. Saul never once pressured me to vote a particular way but maintained that I had the right to vote and I should exercise it. He knew exactly how to get to me. He reminded me about how many people fought for my right to vote and asked how I would feel if that right were taken away from me. Despite all his insistence that I vote, I was surprised when he chose not to do so himself. But I never asked him why. I just made a mental note that maybe one day, if it came up, I could ask.

One evening, while I was reflecting on the past few months and how special everything felt with Saul, I began to ponder everything I had learned about him. He was born in Mexico but never went back to visit. After college, he never worked a solid, full-time job until his recent teaching position. He did not go on to medical school like most of his friends, and he did not vote. My mind went back to the book I had told him about at the Art Walk, *Just Like Us*. His story seemed incredibly like the undocumented girls from Denver. *Could it be?* I had never personally known anyone who was undocumented—at least not that I was aware of. I could not silence my thoughts about it. I had to ask him. *But what if I am wrong? How will he react? If I am right, how could he be feeling and why did he keep it from me?*

SO, ARE YOU UNDOCUMENTED?

The nagging thoughts about Saul being undocumented never went away. After reflecting on what I knew about him and thinking about that book, I became fairly confident that Saul's presence in the United States was not legal. I thought about what this could mean for him and, selfishly, what it could mean for us. The thoughts raced through my head. *Would he have to go back to Mexico at some point? What if we wanted to have a family together? Did he have any form of documentation like some of the girls in the book? Was he working illegally in the US?*

I am Latina, too, but I was born in the United States, and so were my parents and grandparents. As a young girl, I always referred to myself as Hispanic, which refers to people who are Spanish-speaking or have a background in a Spanish-speaking country. Hispanic was always what my mom called us, so I went with that. My grandmother always insisted that our family was from Spain, not Mexico, but she also insisted that we were American and that was all that mattered. I was always a little confused about what label to use to refer to myself.

As I got older, I became familiar with the term Latino, and it seemed to gain popularity over the years. Latino refers to those who are natives or inhabitants of a Latin American country. Since I did not know where my family was from, it seemed to be the best fit. My family had always bragged about how our ancestors did things "the right way" when they immigrated to the United States from Spain. My grandmother was adamant that we were Americans and we should speak English. The only time I ever heard her speak Spanish was when she and my grandfather got into arguments, and she did not want us to know what she was saying. (That's how I learned at an early age that the word "puta" was a curse word in Spanish.) In fact, my grandmother was always so embarrassed about her Spanish accent that she refused to teach her children or grandchildren Spanish.

My thoughts went down the rabbit hole of wondering what my proudly American grandparents would think about me dating someone who was undocumented. Their approval meant the world to me, and I could not imagine facing them with this fact. But I already loved this man, and I had already thought about marrying him.

I finally concluded that letting myself go down that rabbit hole was not productive, and the only way to know was to ask. I did not know when it was most appropriate to ask the question, but I knew I would ask.

One evening, we were at Saul's house, hanging out in the living room. I cannot remember what we were talking about, but I remember there was a lull in the conversation. Out of nowhere, I pointedly asked him, "Are you undocumented?" There was no transition into the conversation, no opening comments, and in my typically blunt way, I added no fluff.

Saul's dark eyes welled up with tears, and he responded by saying, "I knew you were starting to put it together." He walked out of the living room and back to his room and left me sitting there in silence.

I felt so alone in that moment, and Saul's living room seemed so cold and dark. *Did I make a mistake? Should I not have asked? Maybe I was wrong to ask like that.* Regardless of the answer to my question, I knew I should let him have a moment to process it. Although he was gone for only a few minutes, it felt like an eternity.

When he returned, he had something in his hand. He did not say a single word, but I could feel the emotion bottled up inside of him when he showed me his employment authorization document (EAD card, for short). It looked like some form of identification card, with a picture of Saul with a stone-cold expression on his face. That expression was one I had never seen on him.

At the time, I worked in human resources and processed I-9 forms for every new hire who came into my organization, but I had never seen one of these. It was different from the forms used by international students I helped or those here on a work visa. I scanned my brain to remember if the girls in the book had these. I was completely at a loss, and the silence in the room was deafening. Only moments had passed, but it felt like an eternity. Saul noticed my confusion and confirmed that he was indeed brought to the United States illegally just before his second birthday. His voice was shaking, and he sounded scared.

"Have you ever heard of DACA?" he asked.

I scanned my brain, trying to remember if that term sounded familiar, and it did not. I thought back to the girls in *Just Like Us*, and I did not remember it ever being referenced.

"No," I finally responded.

The EAD card he showed me was a result of Deferred Action for Childhood Arrivals, a presidential executive order signed by President Barack Obama in 2012. The president signed DACA in response to Congress's failure to pass The Development, Relief, and Education for Alien Minors Act, known as the DREAM Act. The DREAM Act would have provided a path to citizenship for certain immigrants brought to the country illegally as children. Instead, DACA provides people like Saul, who were brought here illegally as children, an opportunity to work legally in the United States. It also offers a reprieve from deportation. The program, while beneficial to people like Saul, does not provide a path to citizenship and does not provide lawful status in the United States.

That evening, I just let him share whatever was most comfortable for him, which was not much. His comment, "I knew you were starting to put it together," made me realize this was something he had kept to himself for a long time. I had not forgotten a conversation or overlooked a detail; he had kept this huge secret to himself and away from me in our twelve years of friendship. He carried so much emotion with the topic, and I knew I did not want to push him too far. In the end, I did not care where he was born or about his immigration status. I had already fallen in love with him by this point, so how would that matter?

That evening, he told me, "I was going to tell you eventually." I believed that to be genuine and heartfelt. This was not a topic Saul took lightly, and when we started to fall in love, he knew I would find out one day. I fell a little harder for Saul after that conversation. He had been vulnerable with me and shared the emotions he was feeling in that moment, regardless of his unwillingness to do so.

When I returned home, I thought back to the girls from *Just Like Us*. They did not describe anything like DACA in the book, so I decided to research it to better understand Saul's circumstances and update what I currently knew about immigration. The book was written in 2009, DACA was signed in 2012, and it was now 2014. I learned that immigration had changed from what little I knew about it, and it was far more complex than I would have ever imagined. I still did not know how Saul was brought to the US, if he had overstayed a visa, if he had entered without inspection, or if he even had an existing application for permanent residency. I knew I would have to look to him to better understand what this meant and what his future, and potentially our future together, would look like.

Saul's story

CHILDHOOD MEMORIES

Saul was born in the Mexican state of Coahuila in Torreón, a city in northern Mexico. Torreón lies along the Nazas River and has a dry, desert-like climate. At the time, Torreón was known for its agriculture and dairy production. Saul was born in December 1988 to his parents, Daniel and Lizette. He had two older brothers, Daniel and Dante, and his oldest sibling was his sister, Nina. Saul was surrounded by his mother's large family. She was one of the oldest of nine siblings. Most of her family lived in the area, which meant Saul was surrounded by his aunts, uncles, many cousins, and grandparents. Saul's father's family was large too. Daniel was one of nine siblings as well, but one of the youngest. Daniel's family was split between the United States and Mexico. Saul's paternal grandparents lived in a rural area of Durango, Mexico. Saul grew up in a traditional Mexican household, where his mother stayed home to raise the children, and his father worked in pharmaceutical sales to provide for the family.

When Saul was just one year old, his brothers and father were in a terrible car accident. His older brother Daniel, who was just four years old at the time, died from injuries he sustained in the accident. Saul does not have any recollection of what his brother Daniel was like, but his older siblings Nina and Dante do. Shortly after his brother's passing, Saul's mother found out she was pregnant again with another baby boy. Jorge was born in March 1990, and the family took comfort in the thought that his birth would make their family whole again.

But, to no one's surprise, Saul's family was never the same after the loss of their dear brother and son, Daniel. Saul's father saw some of his family members moving to America, the land of opportunity. They were reporting back how wonderful America was and how many opportunities existed there compared to Mexico. Saul's parents wanted the best for their children. Having lost one child far too soon, they knew they wanted to give their remaining children everything they could. Mexico had always been home. It was a beautiful country with deep-rooted culture and family, but they longed for more for their children. They made the difficult decision when Saul was not quite two years old to come to the United States and start fresh.

Saul does not know how he arrived in the United States. He knows he did not come into the country legally, but he doesn't have access to additional details. He did not overstay a visa or seek asylum, and he does not know if he just walked across the border with his parents or if they were brought in by a coyote. In case you are unfamiliar with the term, a coyote is a person who smuggles immigrants across the Mexico-United States border. Coyotes were common in the 1990s when Saul's family entered the United States. Families would pay thousands of dollars to get their entire family across the border safely into the US.

Saul does not know how he came to the US because there is so much shame in his family members surrounding their immigration status. Saul grew up knowing he was originally from Mexico, but he was not aware of

42

the fact that he was undocumented until he was in high school. His parents never spoke of their journey to the US or their immigration status.

When Saul and his family first arrived in the US, they lived in Los Angeles. Saul's father chose Los Angeles because he already had family there. His brother and several cousins had established themselves in California, so Saul's family felt supported. His family left everything they had in Mexico to come to the United States. They sacrificed everything to come to the country everyone seemed to love. Starting over was difficult. Saul lived in a two-bedroom apartment in Downey, California, a suburb of Los Angeles, with his parents and three siblings. The apartment complex was typical of those in the '90s—brick apartment buildings surrounding a courtyard with a pool in the middle.

Despite the challenges of leaving everything behind, Saul's father worked hard as a salesman of satellites for cable television. He catered to the Latino community since he did not speak English but was a whiz in Spanish. Saul has fond memories of their time in California, going to the beach with his family on the weekends, and walking to the local corner store for snacks. Saul, being one of the middle children, was often able to tag along with his older siblings to explore the neighborhood.

When Saul started kindergarten in California, he was only four years old. His mother lied to the school about his age because she said he needed to be challenged and he was ready for school. Saul would not turn five until mid-December, so his birthday was well beyond the normal cutoff date for a kindergartener. He did not speak English. His older siblings were learning English in school, so he had some exposure to the language, but his parents only spoke Spanish at home. In California, it was common for students to not speak English, so Saul was not placed in any special classes but instead was surrounded by others who knew the language and were learning too. He caught on quickly, simply by immersion.

When Saul was in third grade, his family moved out of Los Angeles to

Arvada, Colorado. Saul remembers the moment they came down I-70 into the city, just east of the mountains.

"After all of the winding turns and elevation drops of I-70 through the mountains, I could finally see civilization," he recalls. "There were large, green, leafy trees everywhere. The terrain was full of large hills and drops, so we could see all the homes and businesses below."

Saul's family decided to relocate to Colorado for more opportunities and lower living costs. When they moved to Colorado, they were able to afford to rent a home instead of paying for an expensive apartment in Los Angeles. His dad had family in the area and felt they could be successful in starting a satellite business there. This was in the days when satellites were not attached to the side of your home. With diameters of more than five feet, these large dishes were installed in backyards. Saul remembers the pleasure of helping his dad install these monstrous satellite dishes as a kid.

Saul attended elementary school at Vanderhoof Elementary. It was a typical suburban elementary school, about a mile up the road from the home his parents were renting. Arvada was nothing like Los Angeles. Saul immediately knew he was different and came to this realization at a much younger age than I did. At Vanderhoof, Saul was no longer in a regular classroom. Instead, he was placed into English as a Second Language (ESL) classes. Instead of being surrounded by a melting pot of people, Saul was now surrounded by mostly white children, and he was the only child in his ESL classes who spoke Spanish as his primary language. The other students' primary language was Russian. Saul stayed in Arvada for the rest of his school career, attending elementary, middle, and high school with mostly white children, a majority of whom came from privileged backgrounds. Their stories could not be more different than Saul's, and he found ways to camouflage himself to fit in.

DISCOVERING HIS TRUTH

Saul started his freshman year at Arvada West High School just like many of his friends. He and many of his friends had grown up in Arvada West's feeder schools. It was a big sports high school with a football team that often made it to the playoffs. The wrestling team boasted a player who went undefeated all four years, and many teachers were coaches for one of the athletic programs at the school.

Saul was great friends with one of the football players, Dan. They met in elementary school, and Dan's family treated Saul like their own. They welcomed him into their home with loving arms, and they often took him skiing in the mountains, something Saul's family would never have had the opportunity to do. In middle school, Dan's family had even invited Saul on a family vacation to Mexico with them. Saul's parents politely declined when Dan's parents extended the invitation, claiming that they, too, had plans to travel to Mexico in the near future.

Although many of Saul's friends chose to play football every fall, he was interested in another type of football. He had grown up watching Mexican fútbol with his father, and that was the sport he was most passionate about. He had played soccer since he was a little boy and loved every second of playing goalie. He made two friends on the soccer team, JR and Alex. Both were more or less outsiders in the United States, which wasn't a topic of conversation at the time, but upon reflection, it made sense. Although JR was born in the US, he had moved to Germany at a young age and had grown up in the European culture, only recently returning to the United States. Alex, who also spoke Spanish like Saul and his family, was from the same part of Mexico as Saul's family.

Saul and JR were inseparable. They ate lunch together and hung out during passing period, at soccer practice, and after school. They bonded because they were both absolutely mad about anything related to European or international soccer. JR had a similar demeanor to Saul's, bashful but more outgoing. The two together were quite the pair, and I'm sure most of the girls I was friends with had a crush on JR—something about foreign boys that starts young, I guess. JR and I were in seventh period English together, along with some of my friends from volleyball. Although we all hung out with different people and had different interests, we all seemed to get along. I would often talk to JR about Saul, keeping the conversations superficial and avoiding any discussion of romantic feelings.

As I mentioned before, Saul was young for his grade level. We both started high school at thirteen years old. Like most of the younger students, I was fourteen by October, but Saul didn't turn fourteen until halfway through December. During sophomore year, our peers started to get their learner's permits and would often drive themselves to school with their parents in the passenger seats. Our peers were learning a new life skill and continuing their quest toward independence from their parents. But when Saul asked his parents about doing so, they just told him, "Not now." As time went on, the answer continued to be "Not now" or "Maybe later." Saul began to feel discouraged. He knew he was younger than his classmates, but the more time passed, the more he continued to be left behind. When everyone was turning fifteen and sixteen and starting to get after-school or summer jobs, he asked his parents if he could at least get a job. Again, he was met with the answer "No."

Saul's parents, Daniel and Lizette, were both mild-mannered and quiet. I had known them since I was a freshman in high school, and I had always wondered if that was their natural demeanor or if they were quiet due to the language barrier since I did not speak Spanish, and many in Arvada do not speak Spanish either. Not only were they quiet, but they were also fiercely private; their children were never to speak of family matters outside the home. For years, Saul never questioned them. But over time, he began to put clues together that added up to only one logical conclusion: he was undocumented. There was one puzzling thing, then another, and another. Slowly but surely, the answer to the puzzle came together. He began to realize that it was not that his parents did not want him to do what his friends were doing. It was that he couldn't.

Saul quietly mourned his lack of opportunity as he processed what this could mean for his future. He knew he was likely undocumented, but what high school student has a clear understanding of what that means? And with no parental guidance on how to move forward, he felt isolated. He was at a school with mostly white students with affluent backgrounds. He knew no one with circumstances like his. Although Dan's family was incredibly loving and supportive, they could never understand what Saul was going through. Although JR might have felt like an immigrant when he returned to the US from Germany, he was a US citizen. Who could Saul talk to? Who would ever understand? Saul worked hard in school and excelled in the sciences. His family taught him to value his education, and they instilled in him the importance of going to college. That was the expectation Saul's family had for him, regardless of his immigration status.

The day came when he was to start applying to colleges and universities. His peers were working with their guidance counselors to determine what their future goals were and what schools would help them achieve their goals. Saul did not need much guidance or assistance in determining where to go to college or what he wanted to study. Meeting with his guidance counselor was merely a formality. He sat down with his counselor, and she asked Saul general questions about his interests, passions, and goals for the future. He listed a number of schools he was interested in. His number one choice was Santa Clara University. He longed to go back to California, somewhere he remembered fondly from his early years, with a stark difference from the homogenous reality in Arvada. He was also considering several other schools, including Regis University.

By the time he met with his counselor, Saul had put the puzzle pieces together and realized he was undocumented. His parents meant well but were blindly optimistic. They had always hoped that something good would come their way related to immigration. They were good people and faithful to God, so they hoped that one day Saul would have legal status in the United States. The topic was almost untouchable. Saul was not to ask questions, and they shared as little as possible with him. They never told him he was undocumented, and as a teenager, he had to make sense of his life in his own way. While other students were filling out their Free Application for Federal Student Aid (FAFSA), he already knew he did not have a social security number. This impacted his ability to finance college because federal loans and grants were not accessible to him.

Saul felt dejected and more alone than ever before. As he walked through the halls of Arvada West, everything felt cold. Those around him were excited, sharing stories about their acceptance letters and planning their futures. Meanwhile, Saul was still focused on how he would get an education in this country. Would he have to go back to Mexico, a country he didn't know? He had no idea what was in store for the future, but he did know that if he had access to education now, he would choose to take full advantage of it. Saul continuously heard about his peers going to their dream schools out of state, while he knew deep down his options would be limited. Nevertheless, he still applied to all the colleges he wanted to pursue, remained optimistic, and hoped for the best.

As he searched for scholarships, he ran into many hurdles, with applications stating, "United States citizenship required" or "Must be a permanent resident or citizen to be considered." Not only did Saul not qualify for the same number of scholarships as his peers, but to add insult to injury, he could not even apply for student loans due to his lack of legal status in the United States. He had worked so hard throughout his high school career. He was a student-athlete with excellent grades, but he wasn't afforded the same opportunities as his peers because he was not born in the United States. The future was looking and feeling grim. What was the point in continuing to work so hard when he could not even secure a job? College was looking unlikely, even out of the question. Saul had many questions about what his future would look like.

Nevertheless, he stayed focused on his education and extracurricular activities. At times, it was a challenge to stay motivated, considering his insecure future, but he knew he had opportunities for now, and he wanted to take full advantage of every chance he had. In January of his senior year, Saul auditioned for a role in the school play. When he came home from his audition, he found his family gathered around the kitchen table with giant smiles on their faces. They could not contain their excitement. Saul had received letters from two different schools, and they could not wait for him to arrive home to open them. So they opened them without him. His family knew the big news before he did. Saul was accepted to his number one choice, Santa Clara University. His hard work had paid off! Unfortunately, though, the scholarship award the school was offering would not cover enough of his school costs. Paying room and board in addition to tuition and fees meant it was not realistic for him to go away to college. Since Saul could not legally work in the United States, he could not even get a job to help pay the costs that were not covered. His longtime dream was out of reach, regardless of how hard he had worked. But wasn't his dream the American dream? Wasn't that what his parents had worked so hard for, so they could have opportunities not offered in Mexico? To Saul, it felt like he had no opportunities. He was in a country where he was not wanted, but he did not know the country he came from. Going back to Mexico to pursue his dreams was not realistic. After all, his entire immediate family was here in the United States, and life in the US was all he ever knew.

Then came the news he was waiting for. The second acceptance letter he received was from Regis University in Denver. Not only was he accepted, but Regis offered him a generous scholarship despite his immigration status. This was possible because Regis is a private institution. Since it was in Denver, he would be expected to live in the dorms only for his first year of school. After that, he could commute from home and save on room and board costs. Although his dream was to go away to school like his peers, Saul had no choice but self-preservation. He chose to forget about his hopes and dreams for the moment, and he focused on the here and now. He was getting the education he had always dreamed of. He had found a way.

COLLEGE YEARS

Regis University is a Jesuit university in Northwest Denver, only a twenty-minute drive from Saul's family home in Arvada. It is a small campus, nestled in the middle of an unassuming neighborhood, with large, mature trees scattered throughout. Brass sculptures stationed around the campus honor the university's leaders over the years. As I've described, the St. John Francis Regis Chapel's breathtaking beauty is hard to forget. Saul's Catholic faith is important to him, so the chapel holds an honored place in his story. It provided a space for reflection, faith, and peace while he was in college. The dorm rooms were average for a college dorm, a little worn over the years with a minimal amount of furniture until the students filled them up with clutter. Finally, there was the library. Like any other college library, it was so quiet you could hear a pin drop. Each floor was full of books, computers, study rooms, and little nooks where students could get lost in their studies for hours.

Saul started college in the fall of 2006. He was still such a baby himself, only seventeen years old when he graduated from high school and started college. He would not turn eighteen and become a legal adult until after his first semester ended. He was young, eager, and excited about this stepping stone in his life. He never saw his bachelor's degree as the end of his education. His end goal was to become a pharmacist, which meant pharmacy school would be his next step after completing his bachelor's degree. Saul kept his eye on the prize, knowing it would take excellent grades to get into pharmacy school.

Never one to take the easy way out, Saul decided to study biochemistry with a minor in biology. In addition, he continued his love of learning about other cultures and new languages by minoring in French. Teachers and others warned him that it would be a rigorous course load, but he was up for the challenge. He was a serious student, not interested in partying, dating, or socializing. This decision led him to take courses with students who were also planning to pursue further education, many planning to attend medical school. In Saul's first biology and chemistry classes, he met a group of friends who would be instrumental to his success in college. They were all hyperfocused on their goals and knew they wanted to achieve excellence. These students, each unique but with similar goals and work ethics, became his best friends.

First, there was Vinnie. It is no surprise that Saul and Vinnie became fast friends. Vinnie was a likable, outgoing guy with a great sense of humor. Many were drawn to his fun personality, and he certainly stood out in a crowd. He also had goals beyond his undergraduate program at Regis University. His long-term goal was to become a dentist. He and Saul were partners in chemistry lab.

Then there was Gabe. Gabe was friendly and outgoing. He had been homeschooled his entire school career before Regis. Despite not attending school with his peers, he was surprisingly social and not awkward—quirky maybe but not awkward. Gabe was clearly intelligent and had a strong work ethic. He had a goal to one day become a doctor.

Then there were Sean and Brittany. Both were pursuing degrees in biology. Sean was a serious, ambitious, and committed young man who knew from the moment he started college that he would go on to medical school and one day be a doctor. Brittany, the only woman in this group, could easily hold her own and tolerated all their shenanigans. She, too, was ambitious, curious, and incredibly intelligent. She also aspired to one day become a doctor—an anesthesiologist. Each of them was serious about studying, and they became fast friends. Despite their rigorous coursework that included classes in physics, calculus, philosophy, and biochemistry, the group quickly found success in college by studying together. Regardless of the late, sleepless nights, they continuously achieved excellence over the years.

They established a routine of going to the quiet library together to study. Their unique personalities all came together in a similar and constructive way when it came to their studies. The study rooms were far from quiet when they would all get together. Their collective dry humor, including Saul's, created the perfect cocktail for fun when they needed a break from their serious studies. Vinnie was always the one to remind them when it was time to "take a walk." They would go for walks around the campus, leaving their books and notebooks behind. It was their time to refresh and regroup before tirelessly memorizing scientific facts that seemed well above my head. Throughout the years, they were not always in the same classes together, but often they would share a class with someone from the group, so they continued this study routine over their four undergrad years.

Saul was relentless in his pursuit of success. He spent countless hours studying with his friends in the library but also by himself in the dorms and then at home in his later years. Although he always did well in high school, he began to shine in college. He started to become more engaged in the school as he took on responsibilities as a senator of the newly founded French Club and president of the Chemistry Club.

As the end of Saul's undergrad years approached, he began to realize that his goal of going to pharmacy school might be unachievable. This had nothing to do with his grades; he was going into his final semester with only one class in which he achieved less than an A. He earned a B+ in Physics II, and he would graduate summa cum laude if he could maintain his grades in his final semester of college. The reason Saul would be unable to continue his studies was once again due to his immigration status. He had been fortunate to get the scholarship for his undergrad work, but those scholarships did not exist for higher-level education. With his inability to legally work in this country, he was unable to pay for school himself. And without legal status in the United States, he also could not obtain student loans. Saul watched as his friends celebrated their achievements, getting into dental and medical schools. Meanwhile, he once again saw his future goals becoming more unattainable. The joy and belonging he felt the past four years were just a tease. He had found success with these strangers who became friends, but once again, he felt alone.

As graduation approached, Saul did not allow the seeming hopelessness of the future to stop him from continuing to work hard and achieve all he wanted to in his undergraduate studies. He maintained his grades, and he was the top graduating chemistry student in his class. This led to him being awarded the American Institute of Chemists Award, which recognizes students with demonstrated ability, leadership, and professional promise. Saul seemed to have it all, except the professional promise.

PROFESSIONAL PROMISE

Saul graduated college with honors at the top of his class. That last year of college, he learned his future would look very different from his friends' futures. While they were joining study groups for the Medical College Admission Test, he was trying to figure out his future path. It was 2010, and the United States had recently endured the Great Recession. Saul and his family did not come out of the recession unscathed. His parents' business took a major hit, and their finances looked bleak. Saul was unable to work in a traditional capacity, regardless of his level of education, knowledge, and work ethic. That box on almost every job application that reads "I have legal authorization to work in the United States"? Saul could not check that box.

Saul is a rule-follower, through and through. While others chose to work under the table or under a different Social Security number, Saul did not. He lived all his life following the rules. I have always wondered if he would have been different if he had more privilege in this country. After all, he knew he could never risk any legal trouble, or he would be deported. He did not drink alcohol in high school despite many of his friends and peers doing so. He never snuck out of the house late at night or put himself in a situation where he could be in any type of legal trouble.

After college, Saul did all he could do and worked as an independent contractor with an Individual Taxpayer Identification Number. An ITIN is used by people who do not have Social Security numbers to report wages and pay taxes. Although an ITIN allowed Saul to work and pay taxes in this country, it is not a true work authorization that most employers require. For someone with Saul's skill set, and at the time he graduated from college, independent contractor work was hard to come by. Instead of going to work Monday through Friday during normal business hours, he was working special events on the weekends or part-time hours during the week.

I remember calling Saul every few months after he graduated from college, asking what he was up to. The story always seemed the same. I asked what he was doing for work, and he would tell me "promos." Promos were promotional events where he would do a variety of tasks depending on the event. Sometimes, it would be working a festival like the Taste of Colorado and trying to get people to try a sample or product. Other times, it would be working at the National Western Stock Show as a brand ambassador for Western Union. His roles involved promoting a service or product. I was taken aback by the fact that he was not working a consistent, full-time job. He had a degree and was so put together. Why on earth was he not doing more? At the time, I attributed it to the recession and the difficulty in finding work.

I could not have been more wrong. Working promos was not a job Saul did because he was unmotivated or unable to find work. It was because that was the only option he had available to survive. He wanted to go to pharmacy school, and Regis had an excellent program he was certain he could get into, but without a Social Security number or legal status in the United States, he could not obtain student loans. It was absolutely not an option for his parents to help pay for his further education since their own business was struggling.

Then, in 2012, Saul found hope. President Barack Obama signed an executive order that was life-changing for people in Saul's situation. The Deferred Action for Childhood Arrivals (known as DACA) allowed individuals who were brought to the United States before the age of sixteen and had no criminal record to gain renewable, two-year permits to work and study. It allowed Saul to work legally but didn't provide a path to citizenship.

Although DACA didn't provide Saul with the opportunity to get student loans and continue his education, it allowed him to work legally in a more traditional capacity and obtain a Social Security number. Saul was twenty-four when DACA was implemented. Unlike his peers, Saul didn't have the opportunity to get a driver's license at age sixteen. In Colorado, the laws required that individuals have a Social Security number to get a valid driver's license. Not only would DACA allow him to work legally in the United States, but it also provided him the opportunity to drive legally. This rite of passage that so many young people see as the first step toward obtaining their autonomy and coming of age was inaccessible to Saul until he was twenty-four.

Saul immediately began to gather documentation so he could apply for a work authorization under DACA. He had to prove that he came to the United States while he was under the age of sixteen, that he continuously resided in the United States from June 15, 2007, to the present, that he entered the US without inspection or fell out of lawful visa status before June 15, 2012, and that he had never committed any criminal acts during his time in the United States. He went to the school district headquarters to get all his school transcripts to prove his continuous residence in the United States. Additionally, he used vaccination records and his parents' tax returns to meet all the criteria for DACA. He was awarded a work authorization in 2013.

By 2013, Saul and I had reconnected after several years of limited contact. This was just one year before he would go into teaching. Saul had found work as an interpreter in the medical field, attending Workers' Compensation appointments with patients who did not speak English. Although his long-term goal of being in medicine seemed out of reach, this seemed like a way to still be in the field and contribute and learn in any way he could.

While Saul worked as an interpreter, he learned of an opportunity with Teach for America. In 2013, Teach for America formed the DACA corps. The idea behind this movement was to place individuals with DACA status in classrooms to help students and serve as classroom leaders and role models. Who could relate to undocumented students more than someone in the same situation as them? The idea was that they could meaningfully impact students with similar stories. Saul eagerly applied.

It was at a dinner in 2014 that Saul shared the news with me. He had applied to Teach for America, and he was accepted. I had never even heard of Teach for America before, but he was glowing when he told me. That shy boy with the sweet side smile was in there somewhere, but now I saw a man with confidence and happiness. He smiled from ear to ear when he told me the news. He was so excited. He would be going to Tulsa, Oklahoma, that summer for training.

I remember that conversation so vividly. We were at PF Chang's. It was dimly lit, and Saul looked so handsome. His dark hair was perfectly combed, his belt perfectly matched his shoes, and he looked so sharp and put together. We were just friends. All we had ever been was friends, but I felt something so much stronger for him. This was the same dinner where I asked his opinion about my offer in Baltimore, and he encouraged me to go. I will never forget leaving that night, thinking, *There is no way he is interested in me romantically. If he were, he would ask me to stay so we could finally give our relationship a shot.*

Regardless of my feelings about Saul leaving, I was so excited to hear of his professional growth. Little did I know at that time why he was going in that direction. But he seemed happy, and I was happy for him. He really did have professional promise, and finally, the professional world could see that in him like so many had before.

Long path
to legal

JOINING FORCES

Saul and I started dating during his first year of teaching. Almost simultaneously with the start of his brand-new career, we began our romantic relationship. I was working full time, going to school full time, and raising my daughter from my previous marriage. My daughter, Elena, was a kindergartner. She was a bubbly, outgoing little girl who never met a stranger. She had never met Saul despite our friendship for so many years. Saul was trying to figure out how to balance planning, grading, and teaching in a Title I school in the heart of downtown Denver. You would have never known it was his first year teaching; he balanced it all perfectly and rarely showed an ounce of stress he was feeling.

In December 2014, I knew I wanted Saul to meet Elena. I was fiercely protective of her and never introduced her to anyone I dated. I knew that, if I saw a future with Saul, I would need to introduce them and see what she thought of him. Instead of having them meet one-on-one, I thought it might be best for them to meet in a group setting. I invited a group of friends out to the Candlelight Walk in Golden. To kick off the Christmas season, participants walk down Washington Avenue in Golden, carrying lights and candles and singing Christmas carols. About a dozen of us went together, and I was incredibly nervous for Saul to meet Elena. Saul took a slow approach with her. I appreciated that he allowed her space to process what was happening and did not quickly overwhelm her. He finally came up to her, and I introduced the two of them.

"Nice to meet you!" he told her. She smiled as she bashfully buried her head into my body but did not respond. After the Candlelight Walk, we all went to dinner at Mannie and Bo's Pizzeria. It had been quite the evening for Elena, and she fell asleep on my lap at dinner. Saul just gave me that sweet side smile and asked if I needed help getting her to the car. I declined the offer but invited him to join me in the car to chat before he left.

As we warmed up the cold car and Elena slept in her booster seat in the back, I said, "What do you think?"

He excitedly said, "She is tiny! I did not expect her to be so small."

I laughed and agreed that she was small for her age. "I'm glad you finally met her," I said. "I guess we will see how it goes from here." Once the car warmed up, he gave me a quick kiss on the cheek and walked to his car.

In early 2015, it was clear we were in love and things were getting serious. I had finally introduced him to my daughter. We started to talk more about the future and what it might look like. Although we had not dated for long, I felt completely comfortable with Saul. He always had such an easygoing nature about him, and he was smart, kind, and everything I imagined in a partner. Our friendship of twelve years before dating built a strong foundation.

As Valentine's Day neared, I began to give him a hard time about proposing to me. I should have known he would never propose in such a cliché way on Valentine's Day. Saul has an incredibly dry sense of humor—so much so that my mom often tells me she cannot read his mood. On that Valentine's

Day, he did buy me a ring, albeit a Ring Pop (a candy lollipop sucker). That evening, I laughed so hard I cried as I sat on his bed in the house he shared with his two roommates. We took funny pictures of my surprised face, and I posted one on Facebook with the comment, "He bought me a ring!" While the congratulatory comments rolled in, I later posted a funny picture in the comments of me with the Ring Pop. We continued our seemingly nonromantic evening, although it was romantic for us, by ordering a heart-shaped pizza and renting the movie *Heavyweights* from the '90s.

In March 2015, I began to experience health issues. I went to see my OB-GYN doctor, and we agreed to do some testing. When the test results came back, the doctor informed me that my fertility was low. I was experiencing issues with ovulation, and my doctor was very up-front with me. She said, "If you want more kids, it's likely now or never." She was honest about not being sure I could become pregnant on my own and said I might need to pursue in vitro fertilization treatments sooner rather than later.

I was shocked at the news. I was only twenty-six years old. As I left the doctor's office that day and drove through downtown Denver in traffic, my mind raced. Although Saul and I had been dating for about seven months, we had never talked much about my health issues, and this left me feeling vulnerable. I knew I intended to get married, but just a few weeks before, Saul had joked with me about engagement with a Ring Pop. I thought he wanted to marry me, but what would this mean now? Marriage never seemed to be in our imminent future.

When I shared the news with Saul, we were both at a crossroads. He was just starting a career in teaching, was living with two wild roommates who loved to party, and still had no path to permanent residency in the United States, which meant his future would always rely heavily on United States politics. I was working in an entry-level job, in school full time, and was raising a kindergartner. It seems like timing never quite works out in the ways we hope it will, and one thing I've learned about life is that we can plan everything perfectly and something could still throw a wrench in our plans. When Saul and I had talked about the future, marriage, in particular, we agreed it was a priority to get married in the Catholic Church. Saul knew my dream was to get married at the St. John Francis Regis Chapel. When we first began going to Regis on weekends, I fell in love with the chapel and daydreamed of one day marrying Saul there. But Catholic marriages do not happen overnight, and I just recently had been baptized in the Catholic Church. We still would need to take marriage preparation classes for about nine months prior to getting married.

Waiting nine months to start trying to have a baby sounded like the opposite of what my doctor had advised. That evening, I felt closer to Saul than I ever had before. We cuddled together on the couch in the living room. He kissed me softly on the cheek, and we agreed that, although the timing was not what we were hoping for, we knew we wanted to be together forever and we wanted children together. We decided to start trying for a baby.

Not even a month later, something felt off. It was Take Your Child to Work Day, and I was in charge of the activities at work. I felt so overwhelmed by all the children and bringing my own that I cried the entire way home. I am not much of a crier, and about halfway home I began to reflect on the past few days. I realized I was exhausted all the time and way more emotional than normal. I made a quick detour to the drugstore and picked up a pregnancy test. While I waited for it to process, a million thoughts raced in my head. The doctor told me it would take me a while to get pregnant, and even at that, she didn't know if I could. But I already knew before I even looked at the two blue lines. I knew my body and knew what it felt like to be pregnant. And I was very much pregnant.

I panicked and called Saul, asking him to come to my house immediately. It was a Thursday, and I did not typically see Saul on Thursdays, but I could not keep this secret. As soon as I called him, I thought, *Shit! I should tell him in some cute and imaginative way.*

I ran to the store and bought a couple of cheap baby bottles and a game of Scrabble. I set up the Scrabble game on the table, spelled out "You are going to be a daddy," and placed the bottles on either side of the board.

When Saul walked in, I walked him over to the table where the game was set up, and he immediately started crying and hugging me. For several moments, we spoke no words. I could feel the strength of Saul's emotions in the way he held me while we both cried. That embrace was tighter than any hug he had ever given me.

"I can't believe it," he exclaimed. "I could not be happier!" We were both so excited.

I asked him, "Did you know?" I am not good at surprises or holding things back, especially from him. I was worried he knew why I insisted that he come over.

"I knew it was something big, but I didn't want to get my hopes up," he said.

He insisted that we go somewhere for dinner to celebrate. I chose a Chinese restaurant just a few miles away. I rarely ate Chinese food, but that was all I wanted that night. I guess my pregnancy cravings were already in play. That entire evening, all we could talk about was how our lives would be changing and how excited we were. Even though I was the one expecting, he glowed that entire evening.

I quickly made an appointment with my doctor, where I found out I was due on December 31, 2015. Very quickly, our plans of getting married in the Catholic Church seemed to dissipate. Now we were left to determine what we would do next. We sat down and discussed our options. We could wait until after the baby was born to get married, but I knew what it took to raise a baby. I remembered the baby fog and how fast time flies after you become a parent. I told Saul that if he wanted to have a big wedding, it might be best to do it sooner rather than later.

Not even three weeks later, Saul told me he wanted to go on a date to Parisi, one of our favorite Italian restaurants, just down the street from Regis

University. Saul never told me he planned on proposing that night, but I knew he would be doing so soon. His sister was in town, and many of his family members were in town for his sister's baby shower. So I thought it was likely that he would propose that evening. I wore my favorite dress, in a baby-doll style with nautical white and blue stripes above the waist, a blue skirt, and an open back. I knew it was one of Saul's favorites. When he picked me up, he had on a nice suit jacket and jeans, and he had gotten a haircut that morning. I was reassured that he was likely going to propose that evening.

At Parisi, I had my usual meal, Pollo Al Mattone, while Saul explored something new, a Cinque Panini. While we were eating dinner, Saul told me he wanted me to see Regis University while it was all set up for the outdoor graduation that weekend. He said he wanted me to see what it looked like when he graduated years earlier. Before I knew it, we were walking on campus, hand in hand, and stopping in front of the St. John Francis Regis Chapel. He knew how much I loved that chapel.

Saul knelt on one knee and said, "I know I can't marry you here, but if I can't do that, I wanted to propose to you here."

I said yes, and we immediately began planning our wedding.

OUR WEDDING:
A LABOR OF LOVE

We planned our wedding in a month. I am typically quite a control freak. I throw ridiculously detailed parties for every one of my daughter's birthdays. I plan the decorations, the games, and even the food around fun themes, but with pregnancy kicking my butt, I was resigned to allowing someone else to plan my entire wedding.

Saul and I did not have much, with him on a teacher's salary and me earning even less while trying to raise my daughter as a single mom. We could not afford a lavish venue with gorgeous décor, so instead we rented a ballroom at the local recreation center.

For our family and friends, the planning was truly a labor of love. Saul's cousin, Alicia, a party planner who often throws beautiful, outrageous quinceañeras, took the lead. We told her our colors, and she ran a few things by us, but for the most part she just ran with it. She made things so easy for us, and because she absolutely adores Saul, she gave us a great deal on her services. My cousin and uncle agreed to be my photographers, a service I could not have afforded otherwise. Our great friends Lazelle and Michelle cooked all the amazing food, and their teenage boys, dressed in their best outfits with vests, served our guests with beaming smiles on their faces.

I could not afford to buy a cake, and I really do not like cake, so I was going to opt out of the cake tradition. But my grandpa insisted we have cake and offered to buy it for us. I could never expect him to spend thousands on a cake, so we ordered one from the local grocery store.

Regardless of all these cut corners, our wedding day was what I had always hoped for. Saul created his own set of vows for my daughter. He promised to love her mommy and her as his own. I looked up at my mom, and she had tears in her eyes. Then I looked at my aunt and my grandma, and they did too. His vows to her were beautiful.

Saul and I recited traditional vows. Saul is a traditional kind of guy. We spent the rest of the night dancing with each other and our friends. I cried a lot that day, realizing I was marrying the man of my dreams.

GROWING FAMILY

Almost immediately after Saul and I were married, his parents started to pressure us to begin the legal process for his permanent residency in the United States. Prior to our marriage, he did not have a path to permanent residency or citizenship, so it seemed like the perfect time to start the process. We sat down to figure out what that process might look like for us. At the time, Saul was a second-year teacher, and I was in an entry-level job in human resources. I made less than he did as a teacher. When we looked at the application costs alone, there was no way we could afford them, especially with a baby on the way. We decided to hold off because, at the time, Saul still had a work authorization and protection from deportation through DACA.

After our wedding, time flew. Just six months later, our son, Mario, was born. Mario was born with just Saul and the medical professionals with me in the labor and delivery room. Our families were in the waiting area, anxiously anticipating his arrival.

When Mario arrived, the doctor held him in one hand and said, "This baby is a nine-pounder!"

I remember smiling at Saul and saying, "No way!" Sure enough, they quickly got him on the scale, and he weighed nearly ten pounds.

"Wow!" Saul said. He came over, kissed me on the forehead, and said, "I am so proud of you. He is absolutely perfect!"

Saul is a man of few words. I can often tell what he is feeling or thinking without him saying anything at all. When Mario was born, Saul was glowing more than I had ever seen before, and his silence said it all. He was overwhelmed with happiness. He was clearly so happy to be a dad and so in love with our son that he would not put him down unless the medical staff needed him to do so. I kept hinting that he should tell our families in the waiting room that the baby was here, but he just kept ignoring my hints. About an hour after Mario was born, I finally had to kick Saul out of the room to tell our families that the baby was born and that everything was okay. He had no desire to leave the baby or me, even if just for a minute to go down the hall.

Saul was home with Mario and me for about a month. I couldn't have asked for a better partner while trying to take care of a newborn. He woke up at every overnight feeding and changed Mario's diaper before handing him to me to nurse. He told me he wanted to help in any way he could since helping to feed Mario was not an option. When I needed a nap or to fall asleep early, he cared for Elena. When Mario was cluster feeding, Saul brought me water and snacks to keep me going.

Saul's family seemed quite surprised by how involved he was. His sister often said things like, "It must be nice to have help at night with the baby." Her comments often came across as condescending or unsupportive, but other times she would say things to Saul like, "I am so proud of you," or "You're the best dad."

Saul's family was a traditional Mexican family. His mom stayed home and cared for the children while his father worked long hours. His sister had chosen to continue that lifestyle with her family, and by all accounts, they expected Saul to do the same. But Saul had no desire for our family dynamics to look like the ones he was raised with. He knew my career was important to me, and he wanted to be an involved father. We created a path for our family that did not include influence from either of our original families.

After Mario was born, I realized how much we had at stake with Saul lacking permanent residency. While I was on parental leave, I was promoted, and at the time, it was a life-changing promotion from an entry-level role to a mid-level role within human resources. I remember getting the call the Friday before I went back to work on the following Monday. I called Saul, crying because the promotion was completely unexpected. I had applied for a promotion but thought there was no way I would even be considered. I was still in school, trying to finish my bachelor's degree. We were living in a tiny, six-hundred-square-foot house, just barely making it. This promotion would mean we could finally start working on his application for permanent residency.

Well, as life would have it, you can never get a promotion without an added expense, right? My daughter was in the first grade, and Saul and I had never lived together before marriage, so he was still getting to know her and his role as a father figure. He had pointed out a few things here and there that she seemed to be struggling with. He was a teacher, so he had an eye for these things. But just like any overprotective mom, I thought he was just too hard on her until her first-grade teacher pulled me aside one day and told me she had some concerns. My daughter was not able to do some of the physical activities her classmates could do. Academically, she seemed fine, but teachers were noticing some other social concerns too. They recommended we get her evaluated.

We immediately took her to see her primary care physician, who referred us to a sensory processing testing center because she thought Elena needed occupational and physical therapy. The initial evaluation was not covered by medical insurance, and it cost $1,800. I remember thinking, *Ouch. That's going on a credit card.* Although I was making more money, I did not have much disposable income, and that expense was not one I was prepared for. After the initial evaluation, she needed weekly occupational and physical therapy sessions. More costs. Saul and I knew the importance of his permanent residency, but should that come at the expense of my daughter's overall health and development? We agreed that it should not. We would continue to keep our eye on the prize, but we needed to help her first. Our children were our priority first and foremost.

As time went on, Elena required more evaluations and specialist appointments. The evaluations were never covered by medical insurance and added up to another $5,000. It seemed like Saul and I would take one step forward only to take ten back. Not once did he expect anything different. As a teacher and father, he knew how important it was that she got all the support she needed. He routinely left work, picked her up from school, and helped me get her to every appointment. He did the exercises the therapists sent home with us, and he tirelessly stuck with whatever routine or regimen they gave us when I wanted to do nothing more than go to bed for the night.

As Mario grew and started to crawl, we began to realize that our six-hundred-square-foot home was too small for our growing family. Our washing machine was in our kitchen, we had no dishwasher, and our dryer was in the detached garage. Although I was grateful for the home when I was a single mom, it was in no way meant for a family of four. Elena and Mario were sharing a tiny bedroom, and there was no room for anything. We realized we needed to start looking to buy a home. You hear a lot of talk about how difficult it is for millennials to buy homes. We were absolutely no different. We had depleted any savings we had to get Elena the help she needed, and our options were limited. Mortgage lenders like to see a strong work history, adequate income to cover the mortgage, and little risk. Due to Saul's immigration status, he did not have years of work experience or even a long credit history. He had been able to work full time and obtain credit for only the previous few years. In addition to that, some programs require lenders to provide mortgages only to citizens or permanent residents of the United States but not DACA recipients. We had a tough decision to make: do we buy a house, or do we pursue Saul's permanent residency? We couldn't do both, but if we chose permanent residency, we knew we had to find a bigger home for our family. How could we afford both a bigger place and permanent residency? Once again, Saul's application went on the back burner.

We bought our first home together when Mario was about a year and a half. Our daughter would be able to go to the school across the street, and she would qualify for an individualized education program (IEP) based on her evaluations. This meant the public school system would have to provide her occupational and physical therapy, which would allow us to afford our new mortgage payment without all those additional expenses we had before.

What I learned about IEPs was that the public school system does not provide the same kind of support as my daughter was getting through private practice. Elena went from eight hours a month of support to thirty minutes a month. She quickly fell behind, and we found ourselves back in occupational therapy, this time through Children's Hospital. Once again, we had every desire to start Saul's application for permanent residency but didn't have the means to do so.

A year after our home was built, my daughter was rushed to Children's Hospital by ambulance with a medical emergency related to her other therapies. She spent the next month there. One day after work, when I checked the mail, my heart sank when I saw an envelope from Children's Hospital. I had been dreading this moment. Our mailbox is among a group of community mailboxes just down the street from our home, and before I even got back home, I tore open the bill. I immediately began crying. The financial impact had become unbearable. There was no way I could pay off the bill all at once, so I called and set up a payment arrangement. I could barely afford the monthly payments spanning over a three-year period. I spent many nights looking at our bank accounts, not knowing when we would eventually be okay. When would the expenses stop? When would my husband finally get to pursue his permanent residency, something he so deserved?

Shortly thereafter, our son turned three. We had become frequent flyers at doctors' offices, and we were at the doctor's for Elena when Mario started talking away. I understood every word, but our doctor? Not a single one. She asked me if that was how he always talked and if others usually understood him. I had never really thought about that before.

"Well, now that I think about it, most people can't understand him," I said. Our doctor was probably hypervigilant, knowing what we had been through with my daughter. She gave us a referral for speech therapy at Children's Hospital for Mario. Having been through this before, I called our insurance right away to see what it covered—hardly anything at all. In the end, it would be about $175 out of pocket every week for his therapy. The therapists anticipated he would need about a year and a half of weekly therapy.

I spent so many evenings looking at our expenses. As time went on, I was making more money than when I was first promoted, but it seemed like every extra cent I made went directly to medical expenses for our children. Saul was making more, too, but the cost of living in Denver was high. It seemed to be a miracle that we were even able to financially keep our heads above water. I remember looking at any and all disposable income to see if we could put it aside for Saul. I knew how important it was for Saul to become a permanent resident.

This was in 2018. Donald Trump was president, and there was a lot of talk about a border wall and the termination of DACA. The hateful posts about immigrants on social media from friends and family were deafening. Often, I suffered in silence, not sharing why I was so passionate about immigration reform. Saul was fiercely private about his immigration status. He had been taught that he had to be. Only my closest, most trusted friends knew what we were going through. If anyone ever thought we were just sailing through life without the weight of his immigration status, boy, were they wrong! I thought about it weekly, Saul daily.

I had never in my life lived in fear like I did after falling in love with Saul. As a Latina woman born in America, I never had to worry about my parents or my grandparents or myself being deported. We were all born here.

Saul looked like me. That's why I was initially attracted to him. He was one of the only brown people in a sea of white, but despite being Latina myself, my experience in America was nothing compared to his. I had never lived with real anxiety until I fell in love with someone who could be deported.

NOW A PANDEMIC?

It seemed like we had finally started to stabilize financially. My daughter had stopped needing so much outside support. Saul was now in his fifth year of teaching and was making more money. I continued to grow in my career in human resources, finished my degree, and had a stable job in local government. Although our Children's Hospital bill was not decreasing any because Mario was still in speech therapy, at least it wasn't growing exponentially like before. It had been a few years since Elena's last evaluations, and it seemed 2020 would be the year when we would finally get to pursue Saul's permanent residency.

As it did worldwide, the COVID-19 outbreak in March 2020 changed every detail of our lives. Fortunately for Saul and me, our jobs were secure despite many people around the country being laid off. In fact, our jobs became even more essential than they were before. Saul was working from our dining room table, teaching kids about plate tectonics over Zoom. I will never forget the first time I heard him teach virtually. His enthusiasm was contagious. He was so energetic and excited to see his students for the first time since the initial shutdown. Our neighbors probably thought he was out of his mind one morning when we went out with Mario's dinosaurs and shot a short video for Saul's students about the Mesozoic Era. There he was, a grown man, playing with dinosaurs while I recorded him. His students loved every second of my dorky husband's performance.

Meanwhile, I worked from our loft on call after call, trying to learn about all the new laws that came with the pandemic and how to implement them at work. Some days, I played therapist to leaders in my organization. Other days, I tried to pretend I did not hear my phone incessantly ringing. Regardless of my feelings about the pandemic and everything that went with it, we were fortunate that our jobs were safe. While many Americans were losing their jobs and trying to navigate unemployment, we were lucky to still have our jobs with no pay cuts or furloughs. So when the stimulus checks came, I told Saul's brother that the money would go straight into savings. Dante owned a small retail store that was hit hard by the pandemic. He was looking forward to the business that the stimulus checks would bring to his retail store. In his kind way, Dante joked with me, "Well, going into savings isn't stimulating the economy."

Dante was right, but after so many years of having nothing, it was the first time I had seen money in our savings account since we were married. Saul and I knew exactly what it meant to see money in our savings. We did not even have to discuss it. Saving money was a topic we didn't even talk about anymore because it felt so hopeless, but without even speaking about it, we knew what to do. Money in our savings meant we could finally pursue his permanent residency.

When COVID restrictions began to relax a bit in May 2020, I told Saul we could not continue to leave our lives in the hands of politicians. An election was coming up, and I was terrified of what would happen if Trump were reelected. The president had terminated DACA, the program that had provided Saul with protection from deportation and the ability to legally work in the United States. This action by the president was now being reviewed by the Supreme Court, which left the future of DACA uncertain. We could no longer continue to risk Saul's security and our family's stability on an executive order that could so easily be overturned. As politics in this country changed, so did Saul's and my perceptions of the future. For Saul, the future was always too uncertain, immigration law too slow to change, and any policy toward enacting change was met with resistance. At various times, we had to bolster each other with hope. When he felt hopeless about the future, I would encourage him that one day things would be okay. When I felt frustrated, Saul would reassure me that it was only a short time before we would achieve our goal. He always held onto hope that legislation would change and we would not have to deplete our entire life savings for him to become a permanent resident of the United States. Saul knew the impact that would have on our family, and he never wanted to be a burden. But I could no longer wait, and ... well ... if you were to ask Saul, he would tell you I always get my way. I like to think of it as persistence; he may have a less polite way to describe it.

As we saw our savings grow from two stimulus checks and a tax return, we decided it was time to find an attorney and move forward. The thing about immigration attorneys is that you need to find a good one. Saul's father had poor experiences with being taken advantage of by immigration attorneys. Whether they had ill intentions or were incompetent, we knew we had to find a good one because, quite frankly, we could not afford either of those possibilities. I did not even know where to start, so I began by asking my family.

I have an uncle in New Mexico who had recently married an attorney, Charlene. Charlene and I had several conversations about immigration. If you cannot tell by now, I will tell Saul's story to anyone willing to listen. For years, I joined Saul in the shame he felt as an immigrant and did not tell anyone about his status. But over time, my confidence grew. After the recent years of racial reckoning in the US made me more aware of the terrible injustices done to people of color, I knew I had to use my privilege as an

American citizen to educate others and tell the stories of people like Saul who overcame adversity. Initially, I told friends and family, but over time, I gained the confidence to even tell strangers and acquaintances. I knew Charlene was an advocate for dreamers. My uncle could not be prouder of his wife and had recently shared stories about her success in working with dreamers and winning a national award for doing so. She was not an immigration attorney, so I knew she could not necessarily help us with the paperwork, but I trusted her judgment in finding the right attorney. She referred us to a close friend of hers in Denver, and we made the first available appointment in June.

The attorney Charlene referred us to is a partner at a big law firm in Denver. I looked at the firm's website. Still skeptical of any immigration attorney, I wanted to do my research on whatever attorney we chose. The reviews were stellar, the website was a wealth of information, and it appeared that everything checked out.

I took time off from work to go to the appointment with Saul. Life still felt so bizarre at the time. Because of the pandemic, we were all in masks, and it was one of the first times we saw anyone outside our immediate families since the pandemic had started. We sat down with Charlene's friend, who carried himself with confidence.

The attorney immediately began rattling off what the process would look like. I feverishly tried following him while I took notes in my notebook. He looked at me with a polite yet assertive tone and told me I didn't need to take notes. The firm would send me all the information via email. I did not know if I should breathe a sigh of relief or be cautious about his intentions. I had learned to live my life a little more skeptical after marrying an immigrant.

I put down the notebook and just listened to everything he had to say. He asked Saul about his journey to the United States. When did he come? Who did he come with? How did he come? He quickly moved to asking Saul about his criminal and work history. It was clear this man was sharp; he detailed every step and responded to our questions without referencing any sources. He told us about all the paperwork that United States Citizen and Immigration Services (USCIS) would look at and told us what we could expect as far as timelines and interviews were concerned. He said the firm would prep us by going over facts about each other if the validity of our marriage was in question. His confidence made me feel confident. After our conversation with him, I looked at Saul and said, "Let's do it." No further discussion was needed. We knew what we needed to do. We met with the financial office to get everything started.

The lady at the financial office was very matter of fact. We charge you this, filing fees are that, and here are the other expenses you can expect throughout this process. The total? Well, there could be additional fees or extenuating circumstances, but we could look forward to about $10,000 worth of legal fees. I immediately felt nauseated. All that hard work for nothing. By the end of this process, our savings would be completely gone. The thoughts raced in my mind, but we had put this off long enough. Now was our chance. I put my credit card down on the desk. Saul gave me a look of concern, and I just returned a nod. The initial down payment was $1,250. We would pay monthly for the attorney's fees, and at the time everything was submitted, we would have to pay for the filing fees in cash. I had no idea how we would replenish our savings account, but it did not matter.

After we left the attorney's office, my mind was racing that afternoon. I was doing the math in my head, trying to figure out if I could pay the attorney's fees monthly with my current salary and our current bills. I knew I wanted to do everything in my power to keep money in our savings. As we drove home, we were quiet in the car. It was a Friday afternoon in Denver, which meant plenty of traffic. On the long drive home, we did not say much. We both knew we were doing the right thing, but doing the right thing felt like a big commitment. It also felt like we were finally doing what we knew we needed to do five years before. The fear of what was to come felt heavy, and neither of us was prepared for that discussion.

GATHERING INFORMATION

After meeting with the attorney that day, we received information via email, just as he had promised. He sent details of our payment plan, a list of required documents, and a list of fees to expect in the future. Typically, when I read an email online, I see a balance of white versus black on the screen, but I vividly remember being overwhelmed by the wall of black text in the law firm's email. I looked at the lists and immediately felt anxiety. I am not a fan of paperwork. In fact, I absolutely hate it.

In the years between our wedding and this point in time, I had done a lot of research on what this process would entail. When times were hard and finances were low, I was desperate to find a way to get it done without paying insane attorney fees. I had researched what it would take to complete the process on our own, and I even began the paperwork myself.

The immigration process is all done through the USCIS, and when I visited its website, I was immediately bewildered. I went to the fee calculator, thinking it would help me get a better idea of the cost, which had been the one thing holding us back all these years. I tried clicking a drop-down menu, which prompted me to select the form we would be submitting. I had no idea. It was not as simple as guessing, either, because there were about twenty different forms I could select for the fee estimator. Next, I selected "Explore my options." That seemed simple enough. I found the form I needed, but once I tried to fill it out, I realized I was in over my head. I got about halfway through the form before it was clear there was absolutely no way I could proceed on my own. If I made a silly mistake on the application or submitted the wrong paperwork, we could lose the filing fees, which we could not afford to do. So, although the email from the law office was overwhelming, parts of it were familiar, too, because I had previously taken the time to thoroughly research the process. I was grateful to have the assistance of a trusted professional to help guide us, not only because he would ensure things were done correctly but also because I would not have to do the paperwork.

I was so eager to get the process started that I looked over the email immediately. When I saw the list of documents and information needed, I didn't know where to begin. One item that stood out to me more than the money or the lists of documents needed was the proof of Saul's presence in the United States since he first entered. At this point, he had been here for nearly thirty years. How do you even begin to prove your presence as a child? I was so overwhelmed that my brain could not process what types of documentation were needed. How on earth do you prove a two-year-old was present in the United States thirty years ago?

Fortunately, Saul was calm. He looked at me with his reassuring dark eyes and said, "I collected a lot of this for my DACA application. It's fine. I still have it saved." I breathed a sigh of relief but still felt overwhelmed.

The paperwork reminded me of all the documentation required when we bought our house—tax returns, W-2 forms, pay stubs, my birth certificate, his birth certificate, and a ton of other paperwork. For someone like me who hates paperwork, pulling all those documents together was absolutely exhausting. As for Saul, he had vaccination records, medical records, and school transcripts—seemingly every piece of documentation we needed. My organized, methodical husband never once batted an eye at the process. When we were close to pulling everything together, we realized two things were missing. God only knows where my birth certificate had landed in my mess of unorganized files. And we needed Saul's Mexican passport. I quickly went down to the Vital Records Office and had a new birth certificate printed the same day. Saul, on the other hand, had to make an appointment with the Mexican Consulate to get his passport. After only a few weeks, he was able to get in and then received it in the mail.

We were finally ready. We called the attorney's office and scheduled an appointment to turn in all our paperwork and pay the filing fees. At this point, we had been paying the attorney for more than six months to pretty much do nothing but a consultation. But that was okay. We knew that would hold us accountable, and if we were paying a large monthly payment, we would eventually get it done. It was early January 2021, and I felt so much more hope walking into the law office.

Because of COVID, I had been working from home for nearly a year at that point, which meant that most days my wardrobe consisted of workout pants and a nice blouse because—let's face it—no one can see your pants on Zoom. I rarely did my hair or makeup anymore, but on this day, I knew I needed to dress to the nines. Of course, our attorney had no concerns about the validity of our marriage or us as individuals, but Saul and I have similar opinions about putting our best foot forward, especially when it counts. I dressed in one of my professional dresses, with heels and jewelry, to show that I'm a businesswoman. My hair was perfectly curled and styled, and my makeup was perfect, even including red lipstick. We were in masks, so no one would see my red lipstick, but I knew it was there, and it was a symbol of my confidence. Saul was dressed in nice slacks with a button-up shirt, perfectly accented with a brown belt and matching shoes. He looked sharp. I felt confident walking into the law office that day, partly because we were finally doing what we had been wanting to do for years, partly because it was the first time in months that I felt beautiful, and also because Donald Trump had just lost the election and soon Joe Biden would be sworn in as the forty-sixth president. Donald Trump had been vocal about his stance regarding the border wall and immigration. By this point, his attempts to terminate DACA were unsuccessful. The Supreme Court ruled against him, and DACA remained intact.

When we walked into the law office, I was prepared for many questions and a long meeting. We met the attorney who would now be representing us. Her name was Emma, and she was quiet but warm. It was clear she was confident in our case and knew exactly what we needed to do. Her demeanor put us both at ease. As she was talking with us about what to expect, Saul placed his hand on my left knee, and although I could not see his side smile because of the mask, I saw his eyes, with that familiar look that accompanied his side smile when we were kids. Emma explained that, in total, the process should take about six to eight months, and she briefly looked through the paperwork we brought in for her.

As we neared the end of the conversation, Saul did have one last question. "When in this process will I receive my work authorization?" Emma explained that receiving the authorization to work would likely take six months. Immediately, my confidence dropped. I felt insecure and vulnerable. Saul just shook his head and said nothing. Saul's work authorization through DACA was expiring that same month. We had not renewed it because we were told by the previous attorney that his employer could not terminate him while we were in this process. Emma was cautious with her words, and I noticed she did not make the same guarantee. She offered to write a letter to his employer explaining that we were in the middle of this process, but she said she could not guarantee that would prevent his termination. My knowledge of I-9s from the employer lens kicked in, and I asked if he would pass an E-Verify check. E-Verify is an online system allowing employers to confirm their employees are eligible to work in the United States. She shook her head no. I knew what that could mean. His employer could terminate him for not having a valid work authorization as soon as his current one expired. We quickly finished the conversation, and she walked us out of her office. I went from confident businesswoman to defeated wife of an immigrant within forty-five minutes.

The car ride home was quiet for the first few minutes. I have learned not to press Saul about his feelings on these things, realizing that decades of shame accompany his current feelings and experiences. Then there is Saul's personality, forever my introvert who nearly takes an act of Congress to get him to process things out loud. I waited and waited for what felt like forever, but in reality it was probably about five minutes. Finally, I blurted out, "What the fuck are we going to do?" He responded with complete silence.

THE WAITING GAME

After our meeting with the attorney, there was not much for us to do but wait. The law firm had everything needed to file the case, from filing fees to documentation. Emma's demeanor was always relaxed, professional, and minimalistic. Perhaps her approach to conversations with clients was because we were on a need-to-know basis, and the firm had everything figured out for us. When she needed something, she would reach out. Or maybe it was a "less is more" approach. I was not quite sure. Saul tends to let things go more than I can. He does not ever question authority or speak up to inquire further. I, on the other hand, can be quite assertive. My grandmother always described me as a "nosy rosy." It is a nickname I wear proudly, but I prefer to refer to it as curiosity rather than nosiness. Regardless, in any conversation with Emma, I was likely to ask the tough questions without any hesitation. The more I reflected on this, the more I wondered if Saul never questioned anything because he never felt safe enough to do so.

After the Trump administration's changes to immigration, then the Biden administration immediately reversing those changes, combined with the COVID-19 pandemic, things were not moving quickly for those waiting for green cards. Since Saul's work authorization would expire in a matter of weeks, six to eight months felt like an eternity. Every day after that meeting, I worried. What would happen if his employer realized his work authorization had expired and he lost his job? It felt like it was only a matter of time before someone put it together, and quite frankly, I could not blame his employer. Employers must follow the laws in this country, and there was no way they could keep him legally employed if they found out he had no legal authorization to work. At this point in my career, I was working with legal compliance issues. Much of what I did for a living was consulting on employment laws, which led to an even higher level of anxiety in me than in the typical person in our situation. I knew how organizations I had worked for handled I-9s, and we always had a reminder to check on the status of employees who had work authorizations or were here on a visa. It was not about being discriminatory or unfair. It was that we had to stay legally compliant. Every day, I worried that his employer would get that reminder.

Meanwhile, I constantly did the math in my head. Would my salary be enough to cover all our bills? I often found myself daydreaming—well, it was more of a nightmare—about what would happen if he lost his job and we lost our home. In the middle of work meetings or workouts, I would suddenly be consumed with the pressure of "what if?" What would happen to us? Where would we go? Would we lose our home? Would our children go without? Would everything we worked so hard to build together come crashing down all because my husband was not born in the United States? When I did the math, there was no way we could survive on one income. Saul and I had worked hard to set ourselves up financially. Neither of us had new cars. They were fully paid off by this point. But we had a mortgage, a kiddo in preschool, a kiddo in speech therapy, and overwhelming medical debt that we continued to pay monthly. As much as we both come from loving families, living with either set of parents was not an option. I had a good relationship with my manager. She knew all we were going through personally, and she continued to fight to get me more pay, but unfortunately, it was not in the company budget. It was never going to be as simple as Saul just going out and finding a different job since he was not legally authorized to work in the US. I worried far more than necessary, but I am not one who likes to be caught off guard. Something inside of me says that if I'm prepared for the worst, I'll respond better to it. Regardless of the accuracy of that thought, it is just who I tend to be.

As Saul continued working as a teacher after his work authorization expired, more fear began to build. What kind of consequences could we face for him working without authorization? Again, I asked Emma the tough questions. She reassured us that everything would be okay and that USCIS would understand that he needs to work while in this country. Something felt unsettling about that advice. By nature, I tend to be more skeptical, but regardless of my skepticism, this did not add up for me. Saul and I decided to take things day by day and roll with the punches as necessary. If he lost his job, we did have money in savings that could help keep us afloat. But for someone who had been a single mom and once had nothing, it was almost unfathomable to think of having absolutely nothing in savings. We had worked so hard to build up the little bit we had—not buying new cars when ours had trouble, Saul still wearing clothes from college, and missing out on family vacations. The thought of that money dwindling away was terrifying.

Saul checked his status on the USCIS website every day. He knew when the agency received our paperwork, and he was well-informed on any updates to our case, often before we heard from Emma or received anything in the mail. I did not know how to check on our case on the website. I relied solely on Saul for that, which was better in the long run because the updates were few and far between. In February 2021, we knew that USCIS had received the paperwork and that it was "under review," but we did not receive any updates again until June 2021. When I asked Saul about any updates to the case, he always looked at me with defeat in his eyes and said, "Still nothing." On one occasion, I specifically asked him what the website said. There I was again with my "curiosity." He snapped back at me this time and said, "All it says is application received and the date. I don't know what else you could be expecting!" I knew immediately that something in my tone or the question itself did not sit well with Saul. He was defensive and seemed to think I was questioning him, but that could not be further from the truth. As an American citizen, I had never considered what this process was like for someone coming to the United States. Regardless of what country people are from, their income levels, or their personal circumstances, the fact that they faced this arduous process seemed unbelievable. How on earth can we deem ourselves the best country in the world, yet this process is so archaic? How are there no updates for months at a time?

Our family and friends periodically inquired how things were going. Many friends were incredibly supportive throughout the process, and they did their best to educate themselves on what we were going through. When they asked questions and I told them, "Still no update," they could not believe it either. Saul was a good man. He was educated, a valued teacher, a soccer coach, and someone who had truly done nothing illegal in his life. Our friends were baffled by the process he was going through.

We filed the paperwork in January, and for me, the countdown started. Every month that passed, I thought, *One more down, so many to go.* I guess you could say I was a bit naive. I thought we would be lucky, and it would happen more quickly than the six- to eight-month time frame Emma quoted. But in May, five months in, the never-ending worry continued and became so overwhelming that I convinced myself I had to get a second job to make sure we would be okay. Without even consulting with Saul, I began applying for a second job.

I love to bake, and I learned how to bake when it was just my daughter and me. My jaw dropped seeing the Pinterest parties people throw for their children, and I longed for the day when I would be able to do the same for my daughter. I spent hours and hours on YouTube and Facebook groups, learning how to make personalized cakes, cupcakes, and cookies so she could have those parties too. I thought to myself, *If I have to work a second job, it might as well be something I enjoy.*

I applied to Crumbl Cookies, and within a few days, I got an email from the owner asking me to come in for an interview. She was kind but a little apprehensive. She asked what hours I could work, and I explained that I had a full-time job, so this would be a side job. Somehow, over the past six years, I was beginning to carry the same shame Saul carried surrounding his immigration. I couldn't tell her why I needed the second job, so when she asked why, I told her I had been working from home since the pandemic started. At this point, it had been over a year and it felt isolating, so I needed something to get me out of the house. I somehow convinced myself of this reasoning as well. I must have done a pretty good job at convincing her, too, because she hired me on the spot. On the way home, I took a deep breath, a sigh of relief. It would be okay if Saul lost his job now. I would make enough to keep us afloat. After all, we were supposed to be the lucky ones, right? Only one month left!

As the end of the school year came closer and closer, Saul and I talked about the status of the case. Still no updates, and at this point, no work authorization either. Teachers usually commit to coming back the next year prior to the end of the current school year, and Saul's administrators were trying to plan for the next year. As a multilingual science teacher at a Title I school, he was invaluable to them. Saul had won an award from the Colorado Avalanche that school year as the Most Valuable Teacher. I always admired Saul for the love and hard work he put into teaching. I personally saw the late nights and long days on the weekends when he tirelessly planned lessons that would excite the children about science. He never took days off, and he was committed to those children despite how challenging they could be. When he won the award, I was not surprised, and I had a feeling of elation. He was getting all the recognition he so deserved.

Saul and I talked about the commitment he would be making if he agreed to come back the next year. What if the school found out about his work authorization and had to terminate him? What would happen to the kids? Would they not have a science teacher next year? Would he start the year and then suddenly go away? His commitment to the kids far surpassed any needs of his own. He thought of the students but also his colleagues, and he could not commit to another year not knowing if he could follow through. He submitted his resignation, and I was starting to work the second job. Life felt so surreal, and I knew it was changing forever.

One afternoon, I was looking out the back door of our home. We live in a newer neighborhood with many young families, and we can see the elementary school from our back door. It was quiet and peaceful. Before I started life with Saul, I could never have imagined this would be my life. I had struggled so much in the years before. I felt so lucky to be in this neighborhood, in this home, and with him. I finally had the perfect family I had always yearned for. As I looked outside, I said to Saul, "All of the hate I see on social media for immigrants, and they probably do not even know you are their neighbor. You are their child's teacher, their nephew's soccer coach. When these people think of immigrants, they don't think of you."

DOUBLE LIFE

I n a sense, I felt like Saul and I were living a double life. Saul was extraordinarily private about everything. His quiet, introverted nature made it easy for him. He kept things to himself and processed his thoughts and feelings internally. By the time we were in the application process for his permanent residency, Saul had known about his immigration status for many years, and he fully understood the implications. When he graduated from college in 2010, before DACA was enacted, his options were limited. Once DACA was in place, he was able to work with Teach for America to get his work authorization, and that is how he started teaching. Not one of his friends knew why he ended up in teaching. In many cases, he didn't share his big dreams of doing more. So most of his friends assumed he had always wanted to be a teacher.

My personality, on the other hand, is the opposite of his. Maybe opposites do attract. Many call me an open book; you can ask me anything. Many of Saul's friends were grateful when we got serious because they could now keep up with our lives on social media, a technology he absolutely hated. He could always hide away and share only what he wanted to share. But now he was with me. Not only am I an outgoing external processor, but I also became immensely proud of my husband. He had overcome so much adversity and found so much success in life. I found myself becoming more "loud and proud" as this process continued. Maybe it's because I have the privilege and protection of being an American citizen, but I wanted people to know what we were experiencing. Every time I saw an ignorant post on social media about immigration, I went down a rabbit hole of commenting in back-and-forth exchanges to educate people about this process. To the people who said, "They should do it the right way," I asked, "So what is the right way?" I never encountered one person who knew how immigration works in this country. Something I realized, though, in all those arguments, is that people will see things how they want to see them. And until people are open to hearing the stories of immigrants—the real, heartbreaking stories like my husband's—they will hear only what they want to hear.

With the polarized political climate in America, it is easy to discern how people lean politically. I always found myself angry at those who would post things about "illegals." Illegals? That term refers to people in this situation as if they are inanimate objects. People who use terminology like that forget that immigrants are people. They don't seem to comprehend that immigrants can be people like my husband who have done absolutely nothing wrong. So, for those close to me who were open to hearing the truth, I was open to sharing it. This included people who were "loud and proud" about building the border wall between the US and Mexico. When I challenged them to hear Saul's story and learn more about what it takes to pursue the process "the right way," we found ways to have a healthy dialogue. Saul probably would have killed me if he realized how many people knew about his struggle, but I knew that telling his story was the only way to get people to see that we need a change in our immigration laws and processes. If I could somehow get his story out there, I knew it could change people's minds about immigrants.

The longer Saul and I were together, the more I rubbed off on him. He started to become more comfortable in sharing his status when he felt it was safe to do so. A few years into our marriage, Saul was helping his best friend, Drew, clean out his father's home after he passed away. Saul met Drew when we were in high school. They met as freshmen but did not become close until their junior year. They spent a lot of time together senior year and in college, going out in downtown Denver and in Fort Collins, where Drew went to college. They're a quirky pair. Saul is the calm, quiet, reserved friend, not to mention that he is five feet eight. Drew is more outgoing, has a distinctive laugh, and is well over six feet tall. When they're together, the sarcasm flows easily, and the laughter is contagious. Saul is always at ease whenever Drew is around. They have been there for each other in their darkest moments, and simply put, they just get each other. So I was surprised to learn that Drew did not know about Saul's immigration status. It was the day they were cleaning out Drew's father's home that Saul finally decided to casually mention that he was not a legal citizen of the United States. Drew said, "Cool," and that was the end of the conversation.

As time went on and we were finally in the application process, Saul gradually became more comfortable sharing with people. To my surprise, he even told his colleagues at school about his immigration status and current situation. On the last day of school, Saul shared his story with his students. His classroom was a traditional science classroom, with tall lab tables that seat two students to a table. His school was old, built in the 1960s, with exposed brick like the house he lived in when we were first dating. He sat down on a stool at the front of the classroom to tell the kids he would not be back the following year. He told them all about his childhood and how he came to the United States with his family when he was just a toddler, but that he had never had an opportunity to become a legal citizen. His eyes welled up with tears and so did those of several students.

After fifth period that day, a young student came up to him. She said, "Mr. Falcon, your story is my story too." It was in that moment that Saul realized the importance of telling his story. Although he could not change how the immigration system worked, he was now on the path to permanent residency, and he had the opportunity to do all he could for those coming after him.

After school ended that year, we became even more desperate for answers about how our process was looking. At this point, it had been more than seven months and the case still stood at "being reviewed." A good friend of mine helped get me in touch with several politicians at the federal level to try to get the case moving along. When Saul called the office of Ed Perlmutter, a Democrat US Representative in Colorado, a staff member returned the call. He told us that the process was taking even longer than what we were initially told. He said his office could not get the case moving any quicker, but they could ask USCIS to do a review of the case to make sure nothing was missing.

It seemed like just another bump in the road, but in that conversation, something remarkable happened. The staff member told Saul, "We need stories like yours to be told so we can get the immigration process improved." Those words rang true to Saul, and he knew he had to share his story.

Hallelujah! I thought. He was finally seeing what I saw. His story was impactful. His story could make a change in the world, and he could be part of the change for his students whose stories were just like his. For those blindly hopeful people out there who just wanted the best for their families, he could help be that change for them.

That afternoon, we sat in the dining room together. Saul was discouraged. We still had no real solutions or timeline for when things would change for us, but the conversation with the congressman's staff member lit a fire under Saul. I subtly mentioned that I would like to write a book telling his story.

Saul said, "Go ahead," likely assuming it would never come to fruition, but I immediately got started. In the evenings, I would spend time before bed on my blog, writing chapter after chapter. In some ways, it was therapeutic to hope that one day Saul's story would help educate others. And writing fed a creative side I had been ignoring, so it was healing to think that one day we would have a happy ending to this story. My Aunt Margarita graciously agreed to dedicate her time to reading Saul's story as I wrote it. I wanted feedback from someone I trusted but also someone who did not already know all the intimate details of Saul's story so I could ensure I told it in a way that was easy to understand. I sent each chapter to her, and she always responded in such a loving and kind way. She was one of our biggest supporters throughout the process.

Our friend's mom is a writer for a local newspaper, and she asked if Saul would be interested in sharing his story in a piece for the paper. I was shocked when he said, "Maybe when this is all over, I can." It wouldn't be safe to tell his story until he had legal status in the United States, but he dreamed of a day when he could finally feel safe enough to do so.

One summer evening in 2021, we were having dinner at my grandparents' house. A relative of mine happened to be in town visiting from Minnesota. He is on my mom's side of the family and grew up in a tiny town in northern Minnesota. We were still impatiently waiting for Saul's application to move forward, and the pressure was overwhelming.

Remember when I mentioned the polarization of America? This was one of those conversations that highlighted it for me. This relative began to rant about "those goddamned illegals." I looked at Saul. He was expressionless and did not show anger, sadness, or any other emotion. Unfortunately, I do not think this was an unusual situation for him. He was comfortable being uncomfortable. It was as if he ignored the fact that the statement was referring to him. These blanket statements may not necessarily be about Saul, but they do not recognize the individual people in this situation. Instead, they refer to them as one objectionable entity.

I felt eyes gazing over at me. They belonged to my grandma and grandpa, and they gave a look like, "Uh-oh." My grandparents are staunchly conservative, but they absolutely adore Saul. He has singlehandedly changed how they see children who were brought here undocumented, and I have had many passionate conversations with them to educate them and help them understand Saul's circumstances. They already knew I was not going to keep my mouth shut. I immediately piped right up and made my stance on immigration clear. When I speak about immigration, I hold nothing back. I have educated myself on the processes and the options available to someone wanting a better life in the United States. Perhaps it is my privilege to do so because I was born here and no one can ever take that away from me, but I will always advocate for people like my husband.

My opinionated relative quickly changed the conversation. It was like an out-of-body experience for me, and what I realized in that moment was that people do not see Saul as an "illegal." They feel comfortable enough to speak in such a hateful way about immigrants in front of us because, to them, there is no way either of us could ever fall into the category of an "illegal." As someone who was brought to this country as a child, Saul grew up speaking English and attending US schools. Because of his early immersion and his drive for excellence, he was a well-spoken, valued teacher with absolutely no accent, or more precisely, an American accent. Saul is not who people think of when they spew hate and ignorance about people who are undocumented in the United States.

INTERVIEW
SCHEDULED

A fter eight months of waiting for an update on Saul's immigration case, we finally received a notification in the mail. Our interview was scheduled at the Denver field office for September 14. In some ways, September 14 felt like it would take forever to arrive, and in other ways, we were so relieved we finally had a date to look forward to after so long. In the meantime, USCIS was requesting that we bring additional information to the interview.

For starters, Saul needed to get an immigration medical exam. These exams are not covered by insurance, and only certain doctors can perform them. Part of the evaluation is being up to date on all vaccinations, including the COVID-19 vaccination. When Saul read the letter aloud to me, I could not help but think how ironic it was that the entire country was arguing about vaccines and whether the government had a right to force its citizens to be vaccinated. But Saul had no choice but to be vaccinated against all communicable diseases. Something so simple could disqualify him, and we would take no risk of that happening. He even had to get an updated Tdap vaccination because his last one wasn't up to date. When Saul scheduled the doctor's appointment, I thought for sure the cost would be similar to that of a regular office visit, only to a particular doctor. Saul knew better, and I should have known that nothing with immigration is simple or cheap. The examination was more than $500. So we added that cost to the growing list of expenses for him to become a permanent resident.

In addition to proof of Saul's medical exam, we had to provide recent bank statements, tax returns, and our pay stubs. My understanding was that USCIS needed to confirm there were no significant changes in our household income in the nine months after our initial application and before we finally went to the interview. It almost felt like we were buying our home again. Regardless, all seemed simple enough, and we could easily gather the information in time for the interview.

One other requirement never quite made sense to me. We needed proof that Saul's father was present in the United States in December 2000. That was not a detail we could prove, so we had to rely on his parents to provide us with this documentation. Saul asked what they could provide, and they agreed to give him their tax return from that year.

Our attorney, Emma, scheduled two preparation meetings with us to make sure we were ready for the interview itself. I was a nervous wreck before the first one. We left home way earlier than necessary and were parked and ready to go more than thirty minutes before our scheduled time. I had no idea what to expect. After we parked, we walked hand in hand to the building in downtown Denver where the attorney's office was located. Saul held my hand tight. We had been waiting for an update on his case for so long that it was hard to believe we finally had a date. When we walked into the waiting area of the law office, I saw other people waiting to speak to their attorneys. I could not help but wonder what their circumstances were and where they were in their process. They were all speaking in different languages, and I wondered how hard this must be for them. This process had been daunting for me, and I am from here. I'm used to the red tape in our country.

Before I could think about that for long, Emma greeted us and took us back to her office. With her calm demeanor, as always, she handed us each a copy of the application. It was more than thirty pages long. How could I have already forgotten that she had to answer all these questions about both of us? It was a quick reminder that I really hate paperwork.

Emma told us that the USCIS official would ask us questions from our application. First, he would want to ensure the information we provided was accurate, but he also would want to be sure our marriage was legitimate. Did we know each other's families? Did we really share a life together? As we went through the questions, Saul answered every question about my family and me perfectly and confidently. When Emma began to ask me questions, my heart was racing. It felt like it was beating out of my chest, like in those old-school cartoons. If I were this nervous with Emma, how on earth would I be with the immigration official? Then she asked me, "Where was Saul born?"

This question was coincidental because I had already begun writing this book while we were going through the application process. Just that week, I had started the chapter about his upbringing and where he came from. I gave Saul a confused and bewildered look. I truly could not remember where he was from. He gave me that cute side smile that he always did and said, "I know you know this. You just recently asked me about it." Even after his pressing, I did not remember in that moment. Emma just smiled and encouraged me to read through the application before we came back for our next visit with her. The rest of our meeting was uneventful. I am not sure how much worse you can bomb a mock immigration interview than to forget where your husband was born, but the rest was anticlimactic.

Before we left, Emma asked us to bring pictures of ourselves together for our final preparation meeting. She suggested pictures of us on family vacations, with our children, and just living our lives together. She said immigration officials want to see that we share a life together and that the marriage is a legitimate, loving marriage, not just an arrangement for needed documentation. I was perplexed by this. We had a family together, we owned a home together, and we had bank accounts together. I thought it was obvious, but I understood that she wanted everything to go perfectly. Before my life with Saul, I could never have imagined anyone ever questioning my future marriage and its legitimacy. As an American citizen, the thought never even crossed my mind, and I wondered how many people could pass one of these interviews without preparing first.

In the time between our first preparation meeting with Emma and the last meeting before our interview, I thoroughly read through the application. I did not want to give any doubt about the validity of our marriage to our attorney or any immigration official. Saul had a brilliant idea as it related to providing pictures for our interview. I thought I would just print pictures from my phone because I am always the one taking pictures. But Saul had an even better idea. Every year since our son was born, I have made Saul a special calendar for his classroom. Each year had different photos and a unique style, but one, in particular, was unique. That year, I forgot to update the generic name included in the template, so when we received it in the mail, it said "The Smiths" on the front cover. We still get a chuckle out of that little mishap, and I thought if the immigration official questioned it, we had a funny story to tell.

When we arrived at the attorney's office for the second meeting, I was still just as nervous as the first time. Emma had us show her the calendars with photos, and she asked about them. Some were when Mario was a baby, and others were of Elena and Saul at the beach. Each picture prompted a fun memory to share. I am sure Emma is just a polite person, but I think Saul and I were both eager to share the fun memories as she asked about them, not because we wanted her to believe our marriage was legitimate but because we loved our lives together.

After going through the pictures, she asked how we first met. It's a fun story that I love to tell. She listened intently as I told her how we fell in love, and then she asked when we knew we wanted to get married. I told her about the time Saul gave me a Ring Pop for Valentine's Day our first year as a couple. He told her how he proposed to me at Regis University. Looking back now, I can appreciate the lighthearted discussion we had about how we fell in love. Things had seemed so heavy at that time. We were raising children together, trying to maintain careers, and operating under immense pressure to finally get this done. During that moment in Emma's office, I was reminded of why this was so important and why we needed to get it done so we could continue to have a future together and share more special memories as a family.

After we went down memory lane with Emma, she began to detail what we could expect at the interview. She explained that every immigration official is different. Some are direct and to the point, while others want to hear the stories and really engage with applicants. She told us what to expect, from how early we could arrive, to security, to how long the appointment would take. I had already scheduled the full day off work, assuming it would be just like everything else with the US government and take forever. I was surprised when she explained the interviews usually last no longer than ninety minutes. I breathed a sigh of relief. Maybe we really were getting close to the end of this process. We asked more questions about what to expect and what the official might ask. With her normal, calm demeanor, she reassured us that we had a straightforward case. Saul had never had any type of legal issues, he never worked under anyone else's Social Security number, and he had always paid his taxes. Financially, we were secure. We had been together for a long time, we had assets together, and we had a child together. She said we had already provided the majority of what USCIS was asking for, and if the official asked for any of it again at our interview, she would remind him that it was included in our original paperwork and application. Before we left, though, she told Saul he should try to get more documentation from his parents regarding his father's presence in the United

States in 2000. Saul nodded his head. I was again bewildered about why his father's status had anything to do with our case, but I knew Saul would talk to his parents to see what else they could provide.

When we left the attorney's office for the last time, I knew it was our last opportunity to ask all the questions I had floating around in my head. I had spent the past seven years thinking about this process. As an American, I do not want anyone to question the way I choose to live my life. I had never had to answer to anyone before. I do not do any criminal activity, so to have my marriage and finances so heavily scrutinized felt invasive. I felt defensive, like *Who are you to question me? I'm an American citizen!* These feelings gave me a slight glimpse into what my husband must have gone through his entire life. He never had the privilege of saying no. He could never tell the US government to stay out of his life. To be honest, being married to an immigrant meant I could not do so either anymore. I was vulnerable to whatever this immigration official decided to scrutinize.

On the way home, I felt a mix of emotions—some relief but even more anxiety. My heart was racing again. I looked over at my handsome husband, always dressed to impress. He was so calm. I always joke that he's the calm to my storm, but in this moment, it was clear that he was thoughtful, methodical, prepared, and ready for what was to come on September 14.

Where was he born, Denver?

After the interview preparations with our attorney, I could not help but feel a mix of immense pressure about the upcoming interview and a sense of relief that we were almost to the end. I called my brother to tell him about my little mishap during the first interview preparation. I tend to be one who laughs and makes light of things to cope with the heaviness of a situation, and my brother is the same way.

As I went on and on about the interview, I told him, "… and you won't believe what question I got wrong! When she asked me where Saul was born, I totally went blank and froze!"

My brother laughed and said, "So where was he born, Denver?"

I was silent on the other end, waiting for whatever smart-ass punchline he had coming next. That is when I realized no punchline was coming. He was serious.

"Are you joking?" I asked.

"No. Where was he born?" It took him a few seconds to pause and realize what he was saying.

"Dennis," I said, "if he were born in Denver, we would not even be in this situation."

My brother erupted in laughter, laughing so hard that he was just sucking air. You know the sound—when you can't hear anything but heavy breathing because someone is laughing so hard that they can't contain themself.

Although this was a lighthearted moment in our arduous process, it was a stark reminder that others do not see my husband as an immigrant. Some of my friends have even said he is more American than they are, and they were born here. When many people envision an undocumented immigrant, they do not envision my husband—someone who grew up in the US and is well-spoken and educated. Instead, many picture headline images of an undocumented immigrant driving without insurance. Or they believe the false narrative that undocumented immigrants come to the United States and live off social programs like welfare and Medicaid, even though undocumented immigrants, including DACA holders, are ineligible to receive most federal public benefits.

I had been vocal to my friends about the process we were going through. I had a community at my gym, where I had been working out for about three years, and I had developed incredible friendships over the years. When I started working a second job, my friends were concerned about my overall health and the potential burnout I would eventually feel. They were shocked that I would need to work a second job and that my husband could not work. So many told me that the system was wrong. They believed someone who is educated, able-bodied, and willing to work should be able to do so, especially while we were in the application process. I always agreed and shared as much as I could about the process. I never wanted sympathy from anyone, but I did want them to understand what immigrants go through because my hope is that one day we can change the system for others, especially those who, like my husband, were brought here as children.

One day, I brought Saul to work out with me at my gym. My friends there had never met Saul but were fiercely supportive of our journey. The following week, one of them approached me and excitedly said, "Your husband does not even have an accent!" I must have given her a bewildered look. What had I ever said to make her think he had an accent? She told me she must have mistakenly assumed he would, considering we were going through this process. I laughed and told her I appreciated her honesty and I knew where she was coming from. Over the years, I had come to realize that many people would never assume my husband and many other immigrants like him are immigrants to this country, let alone undocumented.

Then there were Saul's friends. Before we got married, not one of his friends knew he was undocumented. He had been taught to keep things to himself because it wasn't safe to trust anyone. His friends from high school and college had no idea about the secrets he was keeping. I will never forget a conversation I had with one of his friends from college. He was telling me how surprised they all were when Saul did not continue his education after college. He even mentioned that Saul was the smartest of them all but the least motivated after college. Little did he know that Saul had no opportunity to continue but every desire to do so. While Saul was happy for all his friends, he could not help but feel left behind. They were all continuing toward their goals, going to medical schools, doing their residencies, and eventually becoming doctors. Meanwhile, although Saul had found a way to legally work in this country with a steady job in teaching, pursuing his education was out of reach.

Once Saul was in teaching, he started to see the importance of sharing his story. He had students with similar backgrounds looking up to him as a role model, and he was surrounded by peers who were passionate about helping underserved populations. He finally began to feel safer and shared more about his immigration status with his friends from work. During the heated 2020 presidential election, one of his peers asked Saul how he intended to vote in the election. Although he knew Saul's immigration status, in that moment, he forgot Saul was unable to vote because he was not a citizen.

On a similar note, we were having dinner with my grandparents one evening around the same time. I am vocal about where I stand on political issues, and my grandparents are too. But they are often on the opposite end of the political spectrum from me. While we were having our usual banter back and forth on the issues, they looked at Saul, hoping he would act as a sort of Switzerland, and they asked how he planned to vote. The room got quiet for the first time in the heated conversation. Saul is always too polite to remind people that our laws do not allow him to vote and often just stays quiet. I, on the other hand, am the first to remind them that in order to vote, you must be a citizen.

When Saul and I began dating, we were in our mid-twenties. I had taken a different path in life, which meant I had just begun pursuing my undergraduate degree a few months before we started dating. Saul was extraordinarily supportive of me pursuing my education throughout the time we dated and after we were married. Not only did he make sure I had the time to dedicate to my studies, but he also helped care for the children and our home while I focused on bettering myself. He encouraged me to spend the extra money I earned on books and paying toward my college tuition. That meant that, once again, Saul's education was on the back burner. Although I began making more money as we got further into our marriage, at no point was Saul willing to let me pay for his education. Instead, he insisted that I pay for my own. He said one day the time would come when he could pursue his goals and dreams.

Shortly after we were married, I convinced Saul that he needed to tell his friends about his status. I thought he should be confident in telling them that he was not unmotivated but that he had real barriers to success. The justice seeker in me felt that others should know the truth my husband had to face. He always brushed me off when I pushed the issue, but he did tell his friend Drew. After Drew had a chance to think about it, he later came back with, "But aren't you guys married now? Don't you automatically get legal status once you're married?"

Drew meant well, but like most Americans, he did not understand what's involved in the process of gaining permanent residency. We explained what the process would entail and that we were saving money so we could do it eventually.

Saul knew what to keep from people and what he could share. He had mastered the art of blending in and staying off the radar. When I asked him why he finally told me the truth about his status, he said, "You were the only person who ever asked." He hadn't told anyone else because no one else had ever put the puzzle pieces together like I had. He knew how to elude conversations that might lead to the topic of immigration. His eluding shouldn't be confused with misleading or manipulating; it simply was that he was brought here as a toddler and was trying to find a way to make it in America, the only place he knew as home.

THE INTERVIEW

The night before Saul's interview, we were both nervous wrecks. I am a procrastinator by nature, and I was panicking as I looked at the list of documents that USCIS said we needed to bring to our interview. I started to read off the list, and Saul reassured me that we had already submitted most of the documents with our initial application. My anxiety was high. So much was at stake. I did not want a simple oversight to interfere with our interview. Although Saul was clearly anxious too, he reassured me that he had everything prepared and all I needed to have ready for the next day was my driver's license. Knowing my luck, I would forget the driver's license, so I triple-checked that it was in my purse, and I even moved my purse to his car in the garage.

Saul and I are usually early risers, which means we are in bed early. Our interview was scheduled for soon after sunrise the next day, at 7:30 a.m., and was about forty-five minutes from our home, which meant we planned to leave no later than 6:30 a.m. We should have been in bed early, but I do not think either of us could shut off our brains. We found busywork and were up until almost midnight, cleaning the house and organizing things that did not even need organizing. We both woke up before our alarms the next day despite going to bed so late the night before.

It was still dark while we were getting ready to leave. The kids were asleep, and my mom was on her way over to help get the kids to school. I dressed in one of my favorite professional dresses, heels, and perfectly styled accessories. Saul was in a suit and tie with dress shoes. We both like to dress up and find occasions to look our best, but this time it felt like we were obligated to do so. We didn't want to give the immigration official any reason to question our legitimacy, and first impressions count.

When I came downstairs, Saul was making his coffee. I took note of the mug he chose to pour his coffee into. It was one of a set our friend bought for us when he was on vacation. Saul's said, "She is my Anchor," and mine said, "He is my Anchor." I asked him if he was dropping hints, and he gave me that sweet side smile I have known for so many years and softly said, "Yes." I realized he thought I was being strong for him, but I felt anything but strong in that moment.

We left a few minutes earlier than we planned and watched the sunrise as we drove south to the appointment. We were both worried about traffic and didn't want it to make us late for our appointment, so we decided to take the toll road to get there. We arrived more than thirty minutes early. Our attorney had told us that we would be allowed in only ten minutes before our scheduled appointment, so we sat in the parking lot and waited. I looked at all the other cars waiting, and I wondered, *Are they just as nervous as we are?* There was morning dew on the grass, and the air had a slight chill to it, but it was a typical September morning in Colorado. My hands began to shake. We were finally here. After much reassurance from our attorney, I felt more hopeful. I felt like today would be the day we would finally get to move on with our lives.

I had planned for a fun day after our interview. There is a "mini incline" in Castle Rock that we had wanted to visit for years but never found the time to do so. The incline at Castle Rock was nicknamed the mini incline after the Manitou Incline in Colorado Springs near Pikes Peak. It has characteristics similar to the famous one but on a smaller scale. It is a 0.6-mile loop that begins with a climb up two hundred steps to the top of the Challenge Hill. Today seemed like the perfect day. The weather would be beautiful later in the morning, the kids were in school, and we had a rare opportunity to spend a full day together, just the two of us. Afterward, we would celebrate with a nice lunch somewhere.

After we waited for what felt like forever, the doors opened. As we walked up to the doors, our attorney was on our left, always a calming presence. Just before opening the door, she asked if we had any questions before we went in. We both responded by shaking our heads no. Although I had a million thoughts and questions running through my head, I knew she would not be able to answer them.

The security crew felt like the Transportation Security Administration. They kept shouting the same routine and rules repeatedly with no warmth and a certain measure of annoyance. The loudest guard barked at Saul, "What is your name? Who is with you?"

I remember thinking, *Who the fuck does this guy think he is, talking to people this way?* I guess he got away with it, knowing that all the people coming here had too much on the line to ever make a fuss about it. I would typically bark right back when people talked disrespectfully to me, but I knew I had to keep my mouth shut and comply with whatever they asked of us. Saul would never be the one to make waves, regardless of where we were. At the grocery store, the bank, USCIS—it did not matter. He remained calm and quiet regardless of how people talked to him. Saul's parents raised him not to draw attention to himself. Although he did not know he was undocumented as a young boy, he knew his parents expected him to fly under the radar. He never had the privilege of speaking up or questioning things like I did.

We took a seat in the waiting area. It was a typical government waiting room with cold, hard chairs. The walls were sparsely decorated with framed notices of rules and regulations. It was so quiet, despite there being a few groups of people waiting. We began to look at the calendars we brought with our pictures. We reminisced over what great memories we had as a family over the years. We oohed and awed over how much our babies had grown, and our attorney even joined in listening to our stories again.

A USCIS official came to the door and shouted, "Falcon." Saul and I immediately stood at attention as if we were in the military and someone of a high rank had just entered the room.

"Come on back," he said. Our attorney nodded her head at us to proceed behind the official. He had a cold temperament, and he asked how we were doing but didn't show much engagement otherwise. As we sat down in his office, he remarked, "You're overdressed." It was clear he was trying to lighten the mood, but between his bland personality and our nerves, the joke fell flat.

The official immediately started asking for various documents. He asked for my driver's license and Saul's, Saul's passport, updated letters from employers, tax returns, pictures of the family, and Saul's father's documentation. My heart raced as I waited for him to begin drilling us with questions about our marriage, like we had prepared for with our attorney. Instead, he began to question Saul about how he arrived in the United States. Saul did not know how he came; he was a toddler at the time. Saul told him he came just before his second birthday. The immigration official quickly fired back, "How did you get here?" Saul told him he did not know how, but he knew it was without inspection. The immigration official barked back at him, saying, "Well, how do you know that?"

I immediately felt my blood pressure skyrocket. *Who the fuck do you think you are?* I thought. *How do you expect Saul to know these things? He was not even two years old! Do you hear the questions you're asking?*

After more back and forth, Saul explained that he only knew when he was brought here and that it was without inspection. His parents shared this much with him because they knew he needed it for his immigration case, but they did not share any additional details. And Saul was never one to question his parents. Once the immigration official realized that Saul's answers were not changing because he simply did not know, he asked if we had more documentation from Saul's father. Saul responded by saying we did not have anything more. There was more dialogue back and forth on this point, but to preserve Saul's family's privacy, I will not share it.

No further questions were asked beyond that point. The immigration official informed us that he would not approve our case that day. He would need more information on Saul's father's presence in the United States twenty years ago in order for our case to be approved. My heart immediately sank. In all the preparation we did for our interview, this was never once discussed. All I could think was, *How could so much of Saul's fate be in the hands of his parents? His parents were the ones who initially brought him here, and during the time period in question, Saul was just a young boy, not even a teenager yet. How could he be held responsible for decisions others made when he was a child?*

We were out the door of the immigration office in fewer than twenty minutes. Saul was stoic, and so was I. Our attorney spoke cautiously, explaining that we would need to get more documentation from Saul's family to proceed. She explained the types of documents that we could use, and we went on our way.

The moment we sat down in the car, the emotions flooded me. I immediately began to cry, and Saul was silent. He did not have to say anything. I could feel the emotion from him. We had been promised how easy today would be. I had talked to other people who had gone through it, and our attorney continuously reassured us that we had nothing to worry about. We had a solid case. Saul had never committed any crimes, he had always stayed under the radar, and he was educated and successful in his career. I had proven that I could financially care for Saul and our family independently and agreed I would be his sponsor and care for him so he would not end up a drain on social programs in the United States in the future. I could not help but wonder why. Why did his father's presence twenty years ago matter?

We sat in the car, both full of different emotions—me sadness, him anger. To Saul, it was another rejection, something he had come to expect. Throughout the process, he was often hesitant when I was optimistic. I figured that we had hired one of the best attorneys, Saul had lived an honest life, he had a career and an education, and we were good people who loved each other and were legitimately married. Therefore, there was no way this process would not end in permanent residency for Saul. We had done everything we could, given the hand he was dealt. He had been down enough hopeful paths to know that they often lead to rejection because of his immigration status.

I told him we still needed to make the best of the day. We had plans, and we should follow through with them. He wholeheartedly disagreed. Always one to shut down when faced with deep emotion, he felt we should just go home and get the rest we didn't get the previous night. After much heated back and forth, he agreed to go with me to the incline as we planned. On our way to the bathroom at the park to change into our workout clothes, we passed a group of older gentlemen playing chess at a picnic table. As we walked by, one of them joked, "Who died? Are you coming from a funeral?"

I am not sure if that was in response to the way we were dressed or if it was because of the somberness of our moods, but that gave us each a slight chuckle. We needed that lighthearted moment from a stranger.

You could have cut the tension with a knife. Saul clearly had no desire to be there, and I was trying to process my feelings and cope through some form of physical activity. The incline is two hundred steps up the side of a large hill, and there is a trail for people to run down to the bottom again. We climbed the hill the first time and did not say a word on our way to the top. On the way down, we talked about how defeated we felt and how the future felt dark and like more of the same. We ran up the incline that day five times. Although I am sure it took the edge off a bit, the pain from that morning was still stinging.

"So, what are you going to do from here?" I asked.

By this point, Saul appeared irritated and discouraged. He said, "Can we please just stop talking about it?" He was short and to the point, and I caught his drift. I figured I would let him process and we would discuss it later.

As more time passed after our interview, my phone began to blow up. We had the most supportive group of friends and family. Our neighbor had lovingly texted before our appointment, wishing us luck. My mom had called to see how things went after she got back home from getting the kids to school. I simply sent her a text, saying, "Not good. I will call you later." She never responded; she knew I needed space. My brother texted to check in, and I just ignored many of the calls and texts after that. I knew that, at some point, I would have to face the music and tell people we did not get approved like we thought we would, but I needed time to process. When we got home, I finally called my mom, and the moment I began to speak, my voice cracked and I began to cry hysterically. This was not what we had expected or planned for. I proceeded to call the rest of my family, the ones who had been supportive of us along the way, crying on every phone call. Not one of them knew how to respond. They all offered support and said they would do whatever they could to help us.

Saul did not want to reach out to anyone in his circle of friends or family in his state of disappointment. Later that evening, his friend Drew texted him, "How did it go today, man?"

Saul was much more level-headed than I was in the situation. He responded, "Not good, but not bad either. They still need more evidence to process a form, but everything else was fine. Now back to more waiting." He ended the text message with an "ugh" emoji.

Drew responded, "What??? What form?"

"A form that is used as a waiver to show that my family was in the country before the year 2000 so I don't get stuck at the border while they process this case," Saul responded.

Drew seemed even more perplexed after this response and texted, "How do you prove that? Lol, idk if I could prove it, maybe a yearbook?"

Saul responded again, "It's got to be proof that my dad, specifically, was here before then. They said it could be medical records, bank statements, pay stubs, etc. Their tax return from that year wasn't sufficient." He ended that text with a frowning emoji.

Drew responded with, "Holy smokes! Who keeps those things for 21 years?"

"Oh god," Saul texted back. "I don't know! It's ridiculous and discouraging."

Drew failed to tell him that he had prematurely mailed Saul a special, congratulatory package and that he would be receiving it in the next few days, so it came as quite a surprise when Saul opened up a package addressed to him, and inside there was a hat with the word "Murica" on it, a book titled *Welcome to the United States. A Guide for New Immigrants*, and another book titled *The Big Book of American Facts*. Clearly, this was another example of not only Drew's unwavering support for Saul but also a testament to their fun-loving relationship.

We have friends in elected positions who offered to write character letters for us, and other friends who offered to get us connected with US senators and representatives from Colorado, but in the end, the only thing that would help us was providing documentation of his father's presence in the United States.

The more time that passed, the more bewildered I became that so much of Saul's fate relied on his father's presence in the United States. Why is it that our laws are written in such a way that people are negatively impacted by their parents' decisions when they were only children?

My friend Christine inquired a few days after our interview to see how it went. When I told her that we needed more information from his parents, she said, "I am so sorry you guys are dealing with this. It seems so unfair." That was the resounding sentiment from everyone who knew what we were going through.

In a conversation with my friend Leslie, I said, "And we were told this would be easy." I was referring to the interview with the USCIS official.

She said, "I just can't believe they require so much information from his parents. What if he was estranged from them?" I wondered the same. With every phone call and text message, we received support from people asking what they could do for us. Everyone wanted to help but felt helpless.

I cannot even begin to count how many times I have heard people say, "Go back to Mexico," to people who are here undocumented. The question in my mind in response to that is, *How can my husband go back to something he has never even known?*

In the United States, some people see immigrants as a drain on resources, thinking they live on welfare and food stamps, do not pay taxes, and bring crime into this country—contrary to all the solid evidence that disproves those beliefs. All these accusations do not apply to my husband. The United States is all he knows, so how can he go back to a country he has never known and has no connections with? I once asked Saul how he felt about going back to Mexico.

"I have no desire to go back to Mexico," he said. My heritage might be Mexican, but culturally, I am very much American. I grew up here."

RELAX GRINGO, I'M LEGAL

ollowing the emotional letdown from our interview, Saul immediately went to work finding the required documentation. He needed
to provide documentation that his father was in the United States in
December 2000. He had already provided his parents' tax returns from that
year, and it was shocking to me that a federal income tax return was insuffi-
cient evidence to prove his father's presence in the United States. His father
was always self-employed, so although W-2s and pay stubs would have been
accepted, they were nonexistent. Given that this was twenty years ago, many
documents from back then were destroyed.

I could not believe how silly this request seemed to me. First, what does
Saul's father have to do with Saul's permanent residence at this point? Yes, his
father is the one who brought him here, but now that Saul was thirty-three
years of age, his father was no longer responsible for him. And what if we
were completely estranged from his parents?

I often thought about our options going forward. The one that replayed in my head was that Saul would have to go back to Mexico. We had established ourselves in America, I had a career, we owned a home together, and our family could never go back with him, even temporarily. As a natural-born citizen of the United States, I had never had to consider moving anywhere else and had never had to worry about anyone I love being taken away from me. Being married to an undocumented immigrant was a reminder that my entire life could flip upside down if something went wrong.

Saul went to his parents' house and got to work, diligently going through old photos, files, and paperwork to provide to USCIS. He spent an entire day there with his mother, pressing on the issue that we had only one chance to provide additional evidence and documentation, so it had to be thorough and complete. Although they had been in the United States for many years at this point, his parents still had difficulty understanding this process. Let's face it—many Americans do not understand this process, so it is not surprising that they, too, had many questions.

Saul's time was not wasted. He was able to locate property tax statements, pictures from Christmas that year, and evidence of automobile insurance. And his father was able to provide his driving record from that period as well.

We eagerly submitted the new evidence within ten days of our interview. Saul checked on the status of his case online every day to see if there were any updates. I tried not to bug him too often to see if he had checked because he was doing so without my prompting, and my prompting seemed to only raise his anxiety. On October 1, as I pulled into the gym at 5:00 a.m., I received a notification on my watch that Saul had texted me. That was odd. He never texted that early. When I opened the picture he sent, it said, "New card is being produced."

I did not want to get too excited, so I asked him what that meant.

He responded, "My application for permanent residence was approved! They're making my green card."

My eyes welled up with tears, and I began to cry. Finally! Saul was here to stay, and I would never have to worry about him being taken away. He could finally work, he could pursue his dreams, and he could be free from all the secrets and shame that come with being an undocumented immigrant in the United States. Having his green card would mean he could pursue citizenship in three years, he could finally start to make long-term plans, and he could visit Mexico and hug the family members he had left behind when he was a baby.

When I walked into the gym that morning, it was still dark outside, but there were familiar faces everywhere—the same people who had always supported us on this journey. I could not wait to share the news.

"He did it!!!" I shouted. "It was finally approved!"

The amount of support I felt in that moment was incredible. I had watched Saul's complicated feelings toward being an immigrant. He loved the United States, but did he know how many here loved him? He may not have seen it, but I did. The warmth and support that surrounded us in the previous few months were huge, and without that, I am not sure we could have made it through. Our friends were just as happy for us as we were to get this fantastic news.

After that moment, I gradually started to share the news with the people who had been so supportive of us on this journey. Just like the friends at my gym, all our friends, family members, and colleagues were elated, relieved, and so happy for us that this journey was finally coming to a close. I had not felt this feeling of relief in many years. Living without fear was something Saul had probably never experienced, but I knew that feeling of fear only after marrying an immigrant in the United States.

Later that month, we celebrated this huge accomplishment in Saul's life. We have so many friends and family members who were there for us along the way, but with concerns about COVID and our small house, we had to keep the guest list to a minimum even though we wished we could have invited every one of our friends and family members. We kept the focus on Saul and invited those who had offered continuous support to him directly throughout the process. Our house was full of family and friends who had checked on us weekly, and we celebrated his big achievement with a green card party!

I made Saul a special shirt that said, "Relax gringo, I'm legal." I was a little worried I might offend someone at the party, but my friend reminded me that anyone at a green card party would not be offended by such a thing. We could finally laugh about the circumstances, and we could finally share more of what we had endured to get to where we were. This shirt was a lighthearted reminder of how far my husband had come.

We planned a mash-up of Mexican and American cultures. I always joke that food is my love language, but for Saul and me, hosting and providing good food is a passion of ours. For Mexican food, we made carnitas, rice, beans, chips and salsa, and empanadas. For the American food, we served barbecued pulled pork, my mom's famous potato salad, baked macaroni and cheese (we added green chilis for a fun Mexican twist), and banana pudding. We were blending two cultures that felt so perfect together in a romantic relationship, but for some reason, society tells us they are separate and should remain that way.

That evening, I looked around at the group of people we had around us—so many good friends from different backgrounds. Some had been through the immigration process themselves, and they were so happy for us, knowing what a big accomplishment this was for Saul but also knowing what weight was lifted off our shoulders too. Other friends joined us who knew nothing about the process before watching us go through it, but they were happy to learn and be allies.

Some of the first guests to arrive were my Aunt Margarita and my Uncle Rudy. My aunt had been reading chapter by chapter of this book. She had the biggest smile on her face; she was beaming with happiness for us. She knew more than anyone what Saul had been through to get there that evening.

She gave him a big hug and had a large gift bag in her hand. She insisted that he open it right away. As he opened the gift bag, he came across an Under Armour shirt with an American flag on it and a mug featuring an American flag. She hugged him again and said, "We are so proud of you! We love you!"

We did a toast that evening, and I asked Saul to give a speech. In his fun-loving way, he used plastic utensils to tap on the plastic cups we were using for our toast to get everyone's attention. Following that failed attempt to get the room quiet, he proceeded to use a classic teacher's line, saying, "I'll wait."

Everyone began to giggle. Finally, the room quieted down, and Saul had everyone's attention.

"Thank you all for being here tonight," he said. "We truly appreciate all of your support during this process." Clearly emotional, he continued, "This has been thirty years in the making and is only the beginning of many good things to come."

Our friend Kyle interjected, "How can it be thirty years in the making if you're only twenty-six?"

Everyone laughed again, but I don't think there was a dry eye in the room about ten seconds into his speech. After a few more brief comments from Saul, everyone cheered and lifted their glasses with excitement.

When Saul walked my parents to the door toward the end of the night, he said, "Thank you for bringing your daughter to Arvada so I could meet her."

My mom laughed and said, "Oh, she hated us for it!" Dad smirked and gave him a firm handshake. I just smiled, knowing that as much as I hated high school, that's where I met the love of my life, so I would not take it back for anything now.

THE PATH AHEAD

Afters the green card party, the question for many, including Saul and me, was, "What's next?" He had left his career in teaching, and we were in the middle of the first semester, so it was unlikely he would get a teaching job again until the next school year. But aside from considering the available teaching jobs, the question was whether teaching was what he wanted to continue to do in the future. The pandemic had changed teaching, and we were seeing teachers leave the profession in droves. The time away had given Saul a new perspective, and although he loved his students, he realized his teaching days were over.

Over the years, Saul and I had talked about his hopes and dreams—what he would have done after college if he could have. He was at a point in his life where most people are at a younger age, in their early twenties, trying to find out what they want to do when they grow up. Instead, we were finally there, more than ten years later, because of the hurdles that got in the way due to his immigration status. We talked about what to do now. His initial goal of going to pharmacy school had come and gone, and he no longer had an interest in it. Eleven years out of college gave him that perspective. He knew he wanted to do more and that he wanted to find a way to continue to help people. We discussed the career options he was interested in. The two options he landed on were to become a physical therapist or a physician assistant.

Our conversations reminded me of our dinner at Chipotle years before, when he lit up talking about helping patients navigate the health care system. He was meant to be in medicine. Both career options would require a major commitment for someone with a family. Both would require additional years in school full time, likely unpaid internships or rotations, and student loans, but none of that mattered at this point. Although Saul's goals had been more delayed than those of a younger person, I did not want the timing to play any part in his decision-making and pursuit of his original dreams of being in medicine.

Now that he was a permanent resident, he could obtain student loans, which made his dreams of further education possible. He had to consider which option was best for him. He looked at the prerequisites needed to get into either program. Regardless of which he chose, he would need two additional classes outside of his undergrad work. He would need to take Statistics and an Anatomy and Physiology class. Upon completion of these prerequisites, he could immediately apply to PT school. For PA school, he would need recent experience in health care or the medical field. That could be tricky, considering that he was in teaching for seven years. Although he had spent time interpreting in the medical field, which is where he found a true love for it, he would not be able to use those hours. They were too long ago. Every time we looked at his options, it felt like we continued to run into more hurdles along the way. Some programs would not accept his undergraduate credits because of the years that had elapsed since he completed them. Unfortunately, the people who make those rules do not realize that, for some, there is no option to go directly to graduate school. We knew the goal was to get him into the health care field to earn those hours. We wanted to give him every opportunity to get into the right program.

He quickly started applying to work in health care. He applied to interpreter positions and many laboratory technician positions. It felt like he was starting all over again, but this was a necessary step in his journey to achieve his dreams. One day, we were talking about the COVID-19 pandemic, and I suggested Saul look for work in public health because there was a great need for it then. He agreed and decided to apply to work at a lab processing COVID tests. Shortly thereafter, he shared the news with me that he was offered a position to work in a lab. With his typically calm demeanor, he did not have a lot of excitement in his voice or body language, but he had a giant smile on his face, and I could see how relieved he was at the prospect of working again and doing something he was interested in and passionate about. As always, my response was in complete contrast to his calm demeanor, and I jumped out of the chair I was sitting in and hollered, "Yay!" I followed that up with a big, long hug. After the year we had, he would finally work in a field where he could utilize his degree. He would be working again, which was a major relief for us financially, and even more important, he would be working toward his goals of continuing his education and helping others.

At the time I'm writing this, Saul is back in school taking an online Anatomy and Physiology class and an online Statistics class so he can pursue either program, with hopes of getting into at least one of them. He wasted no time doing what he needed to do to pursue his dreams. He is working overnight at the lab, and on his days off, he enjoys telling the kids all about the cool things he gets to do at the lab. Our teenage daughter pretends to be interested, but really, she just loves the time she gets to spend with him, regardless of what nerdy things they are talking about. Meanwhile, our son listens intently and excitedly talks about the pipettes in the lab and the cool laboratory equipment that his dad now gets to play with daily.

After getting his green card, Saul can finally dream about the future. Shortly after the green card party, Saul started doing the math: three years to apply for citizenship, and then he and Elena will be eligible to vote for the first time in the same presidential election. He looked at me with tears in his eyes and said, "My goal is to vote with Elena for the first time." My eyes welled up with tears too. Not only were we finally making real plans for our future, but he was once again following through on the vows he said to her on our wedding day. He loves her like his own.

As for me, I have the pleasure of sitting back and watching this man I fell in love with twenty years ago shine like I have never seen him shine before. The nights are long and the days are busy, but I know that every ounce of hard work Saul has put in will eventually pay off, and he will continue to be a hero to our family and an inspiration to many others. I was drawn to him because he looked like me when we were just thirteen years old, but at the time I had no idea what was in store for us. I feel immense joy and honor that I was able to accompany him on this challenging but rewarding journey.

ACKNOWLEDGMENTS

Thank you to my incredible partner in life, Saul. Thank you for being the inspiration for this story and for living a life of courage and grace. Thank you for tolerating me talking to myself, typing, and over-thinking in bed at midnight when I should have been sleeping, but instead I was writing this book. Thank you for trusting me to tell your inspiring story.

Thank you to my Aunt Margarita for reading chapter by chapter before this book was polished by my talented editors and for believing in my dream of one day making this book a reality.

Thank you to the team of talented and creative individuals who helped me perfect this story for the readers:

Camille Parker, publishing consultant Jan Stapleman, development and copy editor Jennifer Jas, proof editor

Victoria Wolf, cover design and layout

Polly Letofsky, owner of My Word Publishing

A huge thank you to the many friends and family members who have supported me on this journey.

ABOUT THE AUTHOR

Doreen Padilla grew up in the suburbs of Denver, Colorado, where she lives today with her husband and two children. She's honored to be the first person in her family to graduate from college and go on to earn a graduate degree. In her current career in local government, she wears many hats to support employees in her organization. As a public servant and the grandchild of a politician, Doreen is dedicated to the communities around her and is consistently advocating for positive change. An avid cook and baker, she jokingly refers to food as her "love language." She describes herself as a dad joke enthusiast and an armchair detective for all things true crime.

Made in the USA
Thornton, CO
12/31/22 21:33:19

e3f44f31-7f0e-4509-88fa-8b3bbbb5e7d6R01